Illustrated **BUYER'S ★ GUIDE**™

Ford Model T & Model A

Paul G. McLaughlin

MBI Publishing Company

This book is dedicated to Bernice McLaughlin, who has had to endure the ups and downs of being in a relationship with a dedicated car enthusiast for the past twnety odd years. She definitely deserves better.

First published in 1994 by MBI Publishing Company, PO Box 1, 729 Prospect Avenue, Osceola, WI 54020-0001 USA

© Paul G. McLaughlin, 1994

All rights reserved. With the exception of quoting brief passages for the purposes of review no part of this publication may be reproduced without prior written permission from the Publisher.

The information in this book is true and complete to the best of our knowledge. All recommendations are made without any guarantee on the part of the author or Publisher, who also disclaim any liability incurred in connection with the use of this data or specific details.

We recognize that some words, model names and designations, for example, mentioned herein are the property of the trademark holder. We use them for identification purposes only. This is not an official publication.

MBI Publishing Company books are also available at discounts in bulk quantity for industrial or sales-promotional use. For details write to Special Sales Manager at Motorbooks International Wholesalers & Distributors, 729 Prospect Avenue, PO Box 1, Osceola, WI 54020-0001 USA.

Library of Congress Cataloging-in-Publication Data

McLaughlin, Paul G.
    Illustrated Ford model T & model A buyer's guide
        p. cm. —(MBI Publishing Company illustrated buyer's guide series)
    Includes index.
    ISBN 0-87938-950-8
    1. Ford model T automobile—Collectors and collecting. 2. Ford Model T automobile—Purchasing. I. Title II. Series.
TL215.F7M34   1994
629.222'2—dc20   94-23043

On the front cover: On the left is a 1914 Model T Touring Car owned by Jesse and Grace Bonar of Polk City, Florida; on the right is a 1931 Model A Roadster owned by Harold Grizzard of Lakeland, Florida. *Mike Mueller*

On the back cover: Henry Ford with his first automobile, the "Quadricycle," and the "Ten Millionth" Model T, a 1924 Touring Car. *Ford Motor Company;* a 1931 Model A DeLuxe Delivery Car. *Ford Motor Company*

Printed in the United States of America

Contents

	Acknowledgements	4
	Foreword	4
	Star Rating	5
Chapter 1	The Early Years 1908-1910	6
Chapter 2	A New Decade Begins for Henry's Universal Car	10
Chapter 3	1915: A Milestone Year in More Ways Than One	19
Chapter 4	1919-1920: Closing Out a Very Busy Decade	27
Chapter 5	1921: A New Decade and Some New Direction	35
Chapter 6	1923: A New Look for a Grand Old Lady	42
Chapter 7	1925: The Beginning of the End for Henry's Lizzie	51
Chapter 8	Henry Makes a Lady out of Lizzie	62
Chapter 9	Happy Days are Here Again	72
Chapter 10	Refining Henry's Lady	80
Chapter 11	Henry's Lady Reaches the End of the Road	92
	Epilogue	102
	Appendices	104
	Index	128

Acknowledgments

I would like to thank the following individuals for assisting me in preparing this book: Bernice McLaughlin, Albuquerque, NM; Paul G. McLaughlin, Sr., Arlington, MA; Ken Campbell, Albuquerque, NM; Dr. Robert Lucero, DDS, Albuquerque, NM; Eddie Corbin, Albuquerque, NM; Elliott Kahn, Clearwater Beach, FL; Jim Clements, Albuquerque, NM; Don Bunn, Bloomington, MN; Charles M. Sullivan, Cambridge Historical Commission, Cambridge, MA; Jerry Bougher, Albany, OR; Carl King, Everett, MA; Guy Appleman, Albuquerque, NM; Warren M. Little, Cambridge Historical Society, Cambridge, MA; Clarence Schritter, Albuquerque, NM; Daniel Mahoney (deceased), Arlington, MA; Dick Copello, York, PA; and Dr. Peter Rich, MD, New Plymouth, New Zealand.

Foreword

Ask most Americans a simple question like, "who invented the automobile," and chances are they will answer "Henry Ford."

Those of us who have been in this auto hobby for any length of time know that Henry Ford did not invent the automobile, he just had a hand in developing and refining it. If Henry Ford didn't invent the automobile, why do so many people think he did?

The reason is because Henry Ford put "America on Wheels" with affordable automobiles such as his venerable Model Ts and Model As. These cars had a profound affect on Americans and the American automobile market. And for that we owe Henry Ford a debt of gratitude.

Paul G. McLaughlin
Albuquerque, New Mexico
March 1994

Star Rating

All Model T and Model A Fords are popular collectibles. But like all collectibles, some Model Ts and As are worth more than others. Part of the reason is demand, and that higher demand will be reflected in a higher rating.

In this book, the rating system is divided into groups to correspond with the chapters. Similar models in different chapters could carry similar ratings. Five stars indicate the highest rating.

This system should only be used as a guide. Remember that the "hottest" collectible of today may not be the "hottest" collectible of tomorrow. Our advice is to purchase the Model T or Model A that you like the best, because if you like what you buy, that particular car will carry the highest rating and value to you.

Chapter 1

The Early Years 1908-1910

★★★★★	1908 Model T (All)
★★★★	1909-1910 Model T Runabouts
★★★★	1909-1910 Model T Touring Car
★★★★	1/21909 Model T Tourabout
★★★★	1909-1910 Model T Coupe
★★★★★	1909-1910 Model T Town Car
★★★★ 1/2	1909 Model T Landaulet
★★★★	1910 Model T Commercial Roadster
★★★★ 1/2	1910 Model T Torpedo Roadster

The history books show that the Ford Motor Company was incorporated in 1903 with Henry Ford as one of its officers. This was the second time that Ford had tried to start a car company, and this attempt proved to be more successful than his first.

Henry Ford was a man of the people and he had a dream of putting his fellow man on wheels. When the Ford Motor Company was

A family out for a Sunday afternoon drive in a new 1909 Model T Touring Car. *Ford Motor Company*

An early Model T Touring Car in bright red on display at a California Ford car show in 1992. Note the white tires.

formed, the automobile was, for the most part, a plaything for the well-to-do. But most of the people with whom he felt a kinship couldn't afford such an extravagance.

Henry Ford wanted to change that. Ford's business partners felt the only way they could make a profit on their cars was to sell them at high prices, that is, prices which were in line with what other companies were charging for their products. Ford agreed to their wishes and bided his time, privately developing his car for the common man. That car would make its debut in October of 1908 as the new Model T Ford.

Prior to the introduction of the Model T, the Ford Motor Company was selling its own Models N, R, S, and K cars. The Model N, Model R, and Model S cars were small Runabouts, powered by four-cylinder engines; the Model K was available as a Roadster or a Touring Car, powered by a six-cylinder engine. Prices ranged from $600 for the Model N to $2,800 for the Model K. However, few people could afford $2,800 for any car in 1908 and Ford didn't sell many Model Ks.

From October through December of 1908, 300 or so Model T Fords were produced in Ford's Piquette Avenue assembly plant in Detroit. Ford called these new cars 1909 models, but some Model T fanciers like to call them 1908 Model Ts.

The new Model T Ford wasn't out for too long before Henry Ford decided to make some changes. Sometime in late February or early March 1909, after approximately 1,000 Model Ts had been built, Ford made his first major change to his beloved Model T. These first cars had two separate control levers on the floor and two separate floor pedals. One lever was for the hand brake and the other was for se-

Not all Model T Fords have been restored to factory fresh condition as Henry Ford originally built them. Quite a few of them have been turned into sporty "Speedsters" like the one shown here.

Here is an example of a Model T Tourabout produced in 1909 or 1910. It's a sporty looking car, isn't it?

lecting reverse gear. One pedal controlled the service brake and the other worked the low/high speed clutch. The reverse lever was gone and here were now three pedals on the floor: one for the clutch, one for the brake, and one controlling the reverse gear band in the transmission.

The engine blocks of these early Model Ts (and an additional 1,500 or so) were slightly shorter than those built after May 1909. Ford noted these changes and referred to cars built with the two-pedal/two-lever system as early 1909 cars, and those with the upgraded changes as new and improved 1909 models.

In 1909, Model T buyers had a choice of six models. There was the Model T Touring Car priced at $950, the Runabout for $825, the Coupe at $950, the Landaulet at $950, the Tourabout at $850, and for the ritzy, the Town Car priced at $1,000. Tourabout was like a Touring Car except that its body had no doors, while the Touring Car had doors on the rear of its body. Both these cars and the Runabout were open cars with folding tops.

In a similar vein, the Landaulet was just like a Town Car, except its driver's compartment was completely open, while the Town Car driver had some protection from the elements. Both cars featured enclosed and richly appointed passenger compartments. These cars were ordered by quite a few cab drivers, who liked them for their separated areas. The Town Car, was the most luxurious version of the Model T. For a price of $1,000 the Town Car buyer received a car with a windshield and top to protect the driver and a separate, completely enclosed, rear compartment for passengers. Rich appointments throughout added a little more class to this Model T.

Except for some Touring Cars with aluminum bodies, these early model cars came equipped with wooden bodies. They were offered in black, red, green, blue, and light and dark gray, and came equipped with brass radiators, bulb horns, and other pieces, and kerosene-fired cowl and taillights.

The Model T used a 176.7ci four-cylinder engine that produced about 20hp, much like the other cars of that period. Starting the car required the use of a handcrank, and ignition was provided by a magneto arrangement inside the transmission case. Power was fed from this magneto to a commutator, a vibrator, and a spark coil for each cylinder, which in turn fired a spark plug. By today's standards it was primitive, but it worked pretty well.

In the early days, the Model T wasn't

Prior to the release of the Model T Ford in 1908, the Ford Motor Company was building cars like this Model K Touring Car.

This Saturday Evening Post ad, dated March 28, 1910, talks about the Model T in terms of quality and low price. It also talks about weight and other interesting points pertaining to the Model T Ford. *Jerry Bougher Ads*

equipped with headlights, but a running change during the 1909 model year Ford offered a headlamp option for Model T drivers who wanted to venture out after sundown.

These brass-encased headlights were powered by a gas that was created in a brass generator on the left running board. This two-stage generator carried pieces of carbide in its bottom and water in the top. When droplets of water from the upper area were allowed to come into contact with the carbide below, a chemical reaction produced a gas, which was then fed to the headlights via a hose.

1909, Henry Ford didn't have access to a wide variety of advertising media to promote his new Model T, so he promoted his cars the same way others promoted theirs: by exposing them to rugged tests to prove their mettle. One such test was the 1909 transcontinental race that ran between New York and Seattle. Ford entered two cars in this race, and they finished in first and second places. Newspapers carried the results of this race from coast to coast. Sometime after the race results were in, the winning car was disqualified, but by then, Henry Ford and his Model T were well on their way. With the popularity of the Model T growing by leaps and bounds, the Ford Motor Company needed more assembly space, and the next year moved operations from Piquette Avenue to a new, larger facility in Highland Park, Michigan—just as production and demand for the Model T increased from 10,600 units to more than 18,600. Within three years or so, production would top the 168,000 mark. Ford added a couple of new Runabout models to the Model T line in 1910. The first, a rakish-looking sporty model was called the Torpedo, available for $900. The other new Runabout was aimed at businessmen and was priced very reasonably at $650. Ford raised the prices on all 1910 models $75 to $200.

Chapter 2

A New Decade Begins for Henry's Universal Car

★★★★	1911 Model T Runabout
★★★★1/2	1911-1912 Model T Torpedo Roadster
★★★★	1911-1914 Model T Touring Car
★★★★1/2	1911 Model T Tourabout
★★★	1911-1914 Model T Coupe
★★★1/2	1911-1914 Model T Town Car
★★★★	1911-1912 Model T Commercial Roadster
★★★1/2	1911-1912 Model T Delivery Van
★★★★	1912-1914 Model T Roadster
★★★★	1914 Model T Coupelet
	1911-1914 Model T Sportster

The Model T was well on the way to becoming the "Universal Car" Henry Ford had dreamed of. one. Production of the Model T began in Canada at about the same time it did in the

A Model T Touring Car getting ready to take another spin at an old car tour in New Mexico in 1990.

On the right a Model T Torpedo Roadster, and on the left a Model T Speedster at a Ford car show in the 1980s.

United States, and from Canada, Model Ts were shipped all over the world. Wanting to widen the Model T's horizons even farther, in 1910, Henry Ford authorized the formation of the Ford Motor Company Ltd. of Great Britain, and production of Model T Fords began in Manchester, England, the next year. The Ford Motor Company Ltd. of Great Britain would be allowed to ship cars into Europe. Those involved with production knew the Manchester facility would run out of capacity soon and began planning a larger assembly plant near Dagenham, England, to meet the expected future demand for Ford products in Europe.

In the United States, the big news concerning Ford's "Flivver" this year was that all Model Ts now came with steel bodies instead of wood and aluminum. Changes were also made to the engine, transmission, and other assorted pieces of the running gear.

Ford once again offered the Commercial Roadster for businessmen who needed a light-duty delivery vehicle. The Commercial Roadster, or Runabout, came with a removable rear seat nicknamed the "mother-in-law seat," which could be easily removed and replaced by all sorts of bodies offered through the aftermarket. Most of these aftermarket bodies were nothing more than wooden boxes, and like the Model T itself were simple and straightforward.

Late in the 1911 model year, Henry Ford released a new model called the Model T Delivery Car, priced at $700 and equipped with gas-powered headlights, a brass bulb horn, and kerosene-fired cowl and taillights. Soon after these vehicles made their debut, they earned the nickname "pie wagons" because they were so popular with bakeries. These vehicles were carried in regular Ford catalogs, but Ford didn't build their bodies. Ford bought these bodies from a variety of sources and each manufacturer built his bodies to his

A Model T Speedster. Note bucket seats, oval gas tank, and a modern taillight.

own specifications, so although they looked similar from a distance, no two of them were exactly alike.

One of the most popular Model T Fords in 1911 was the sporty Torpedo Roadster. The Torpedo used a unique body that sat lower than a regular Model T Roadster body because its gas tank had been taken out from under the driver's seat and relocated the rear of the body. The Torpedo also used a rakish-looking windshield frame.

The Touring Car, Runabout, Coupe, and the ritzy Town Car were all still in the Model T catalogs this year, as was the Model T Stripped Chassis for those who wanted to mount their own bodies on a Model T frame.

The new 1912 Model T Fords made their debut in October 1911 with quite a few changes, including a new model and lower prices. This new model was called a Foredoor Touring Car., "Fore" meaning that there were doors on the front of the car rather than no front doors, as was done in the regular Touring Car. Cars built in the United States had only three functional doors, with the fourth door actually being only a stamping in the body sheet metal, whereas cars built in Canada came with four functional doors because that was the way the Canadian government wanted them built. A Foredoor buyer could remove its doors if he wanted to turn his car into a regular Touring model. For those who really didn't care whether their Touring Cars had four doors, Ford offered the standard Touring Car, lowering its price from $780 to $690 this year. Ford also started to refer to these cars as its Open Front Touring Cars.

A couple of pretty young ladies admire a Model T Roadster.

An early Model T engine compartment showing intake and exhaust manifolds, and brass plated cowl and headlamps.

Another model that received quite a price reduction this year was the Town Car, now available for $900. Just a year before, the same car would have cost $1,200. The Town Car at $900 was probably the best bargain to be found in the Model T lineup this year, featuring a car that came equipped with a richly appointed interior, kerosene-fired cowl and taillights, gas-fired headlights, Landau top irons, lots of brass trim, a speedometer, tool kit, and other niceties. There wasn't too much more you could get on a car in 1912.

Ford also redesigned the Torpedo Roadster this year, erasing some of the sporty character previously found on this model. It now carried a regular Roadster body and a regular Open Front Touring Car windshield, and the unique, rakish-looking windshield frame was replaced by an ordinary unit. Buyers who preferred the looks of the earlier car bought a stripped-down chassis and had an aftermarket sporty car body installed. These bodies were available from a wide variety of sources and most were priced between $70 and $75. Cars with this type of body were called Speedsters;. for about the same price of a Model T Torpedo Roadster, you could have a really sporty-looking automobile. Henry Ford must have seen the writing on the wall, because this would be the last year for the Model T Torpedo Roadster.

The Commercial Roadster and the Delivery Car were still popular with businessmen this year, as was the stripped-down Model T chassis. One of the most popular Commercial conversions at this time was to remove the rear seat of a Commercial Roadster and replace it with a pickup box body.

Model T production this year increased by 44,000 units over the same time period of the year before. More than 78,000 Model T

Though Ford didn't offer a Model T Ford pickup in 1912, aftermarket suppliers offered all sorts of bodies that could be bolted to the Model T, as this pickup shows. *Elliott Kahn photo*

A white-tired 1912 Model T Speedster shares center stage with a sporty looking 1968 Mustang fastback.

A couple of Model Ts parked side by side at a Ford car show in the late eighties.

A bright orange paint job graces the exterior of this Model T Speedster. Note large driving light flanked by two circular windshields.

Another Brass Era Model T Ford Touring Car. This one is equipped with some auxiliary oil, gas, and water cans on its runningboard.

Model T Touring Cars, like this 1914 model, look good with their tops either up or down. This car has also been fitted with a set of more modern turning signal lamps to make it safer to operate on the streets today.

How would you like to own this black Model T Touring Car? Note the brass plated trim on the radiator shell, horn, and mirror.

White tires really brighten up the looks of this 1914 Model T Touring Ca,r wouldn't you say? *Elliott Kahn photo*

Lots of brass-plated trim can be found on early Model T Touring Cars like this bright red example on display in California. Plated items include windshield frame and rods, cowl lamps, hub caps, headlights, horn, radiator shell, and radiator cap.

Fords left the assembly lines this year.

Henry Ford was on an austerity kick in late 1912 and nowhere was that more evident than in the new 1913 Model T Fords which made their debut in November of this year. Most of their brass-trimmed pieces were replaced by painted pieces with a little brass trim. A case in point: The Open Front Touring Car windshield frame used before was made of brass and really added to the looks of the car. Now that same frame was made out of steel and painted and gave a stark appearance. Another change that affected the cost of producing the Model T was trimming the door panels of the Open Front Touring Cars in leatherette, instead of leather, which had been used previously. The seats themselves were still trimmed in real leather but that would also change in the next couple of years.

During the model year, Ford made some other changes to the Model T, including redesigning a new "turtle back" rear deck treatment for the Roadsters and Runabouts. Ford also started to replace the wooden coil boxes used on earlier Model Ts with steel boxes.

Henry Ford decided to pass along some of the savings gained from lowering his production costs to his customers, who in turn bought even more Model Ts this year—in fact, more than all the Model Ts built before 1913. Production shot up to more than 168,000 units by model year's end, and Ford's profits for this selling period alone topped $25 million.

The Ford Motor Company Ltd. of Great Britain opened a branch assembly plant in Bordeaux, France, to serve the French market, and the Walkerville, Ontario, Canada, assembly plant exported Model Ts to India, Australia, South Africa, and New Zealand. "Henry's Lizzie" was becoming more of a Universal Car with each passing day.

Henry Ford had offered his Model T Ford in a variety of colors, but in 1914 announced that henceforth his Model Ts would be available in "any color as long as it is black." This "all-black" policy would remain in effect for the next decade.

Other changes this year included some minor design revisions and the phasing out of the old acetylene gas-powered headlight system. These headlights and the running board generator that powered them were replaced by a more modern electrical system that was connected to the magneto contacts on the transmission case.

This Model T Speedster is all decked out as an early model racer with a stand-alone, runningboard-mounted driving light, "v'd" radiator shell, special fuel tank, and a plated hood.

This early Model T hot rod features a modern powerplant, brakes, wheels, tires, and sits quite a bit lower than an original example.

Ford did offer another new model for his customers this year: the Coupelet. The Coupelet was Ford's first attempt at producing a real convertible model. These cars featured a retractable fabric-lined top and plate glass windows in the doors. Like the top, these windows could be raised or lowered at will and offered the coziness of a closed coupe and open air freedom. The plate glass windows provided more protection from the elements than the canvas and plastic windows offered for the regular Open Front Touring Cars.

On January 5, 1914, Henry Ford startled the business world by announcing that effective January 12 he was raising the salaries of his plant workers to a wage rate of $5 per 8hr workday. That much of a raise in 1914 amounted to twice what a factory worker made, and the Highland Park plant was besieged with workers looking for jobs with Ford. Ford didn't make this offer on purely humanistic terms. Ford figured that with a little more money in their pockets, his workers would be happier—and therefore more productive and more likely to buy a new Ford.

Another reason Ford sold more cars in 1914 might have had something to do with the "$50 Rebate Program" introduced this year. This rebate program, the first of its kind and a forerunner of today's rebates, was pretty simple in scope. Ford promised new Model T buyers in 1914 that if he sold more than 300,000 cars this year, he would send them each a $50 check once the sales figures were tallied. Ford sold 308,000 cars this year and, true to his word, mailed 308,000 $50 checks. This deal alone cost Ford more than $15,000,000, but his profits for that year totaled more than $30,000,000.

Key to this record production was the implementation of the moving assembly line at Ford's Highland Park plant. The moving assembly line brought the work to the workers, greatly reducing the time and effort that went into car building. Ford workers were building Model T Fords so fast now that they were running out of storage room around the plant. Also in 1914, Ford opened two new plants in Texas: one in Dallas and one in Houston. These plants would go a long way in helping to meet the demand for the Model T in the Southwest.

In a further move to boost sales, Ford lowered Model T prices twice this year. Ford was on a roll now, and within five years had become the world's number one automobile manufacturer.

Brass plated horn, and black painted cowl lamp as found on Model T Fords in the mid-teens.

Interest in camping was starting to pick up in the 'teens when this picture was taken. Pat Nunn's grandfather, a Ford dealer in Springerville, Arizona, snapped this picture of a Model T and another car on a local camping trip in 1915. *Pat Nunn photo*

Chapter 3

1915: A Milestone Year in More Ways Than One

★★★★1/2	1915 Model T Roadster/Runabout
★★★★	1915 Model T Touring Car
★★★★	1915 Model T Convertible
★★★★★	1915-1916 Model T Town Car
★★★★1/2	1915 Model T Taxicab
★★★★	1915 Model T Center Door Sedan
★★★1/2	1916-1918 Model T Center Door Sedan
★★★1/2	1916-1918 Model T Runabout
★★★1/2	1916-1918 Model T Touring Car
★★★★1/2	1917-1918 Model T Town Car
★★★★	1916-1918 Model T Coupelet
★★★1/2	1917-1918 Model T Coupe
★★★★	1915-1918 Model T Sportster

If there ever was a milestone year for Model T Fords, 1915 had to be it.

Demand for the Model T was still very high, and to meet that demand better, Ford opened new assembly plants in Atlanta, Georgia; Cincinnati, Ohio; Indianapolis, Indiana; and Pittsburgh, Pennsylvania. The added plant capacity helped Ford to produce more than 500,000 cars this year—including the "Millionth Model T" that left the assembly line in September of that year.

The Model T featured quite a few appearance changes this year, including a redesigned cowl and curved rear fenders. The cherrywood dashboard used in previous years was replaced by a pressed-steel unit, and the formerly squared cowl lights were now round. Louvers were punched in the hood's sides to aid in cooling, leatherette replaced real leather for the seat covers on the Open Front Touring Car, and the old "bulb" horn was replaced with a more modern Klaxon type.

It wasn't common knowledge, but Ford also offered two tread widths for the Model T: the standard 56in-wide tread and 60in-wide tread for traveling in the wagon ruts along dirt roads. Wagons in the Southeast had wider axles than was the norm in other areas, and drivers of cars with narrower treads faced all sorts of problems with the ride, track, and handling. So Henry Ford gave these people something they needed. However, this would be the last year that the Model T would be available in two tread widths.

As an added bonus this year, Ford offered two new closed models in his Model T lineup: the Center Door Sedan and the Taxicab. The Center Door Sedan featured one door per side in the middle of the body, which offered access into both the front and rear areas of the interior. Model Ts had been used as taxicabs before but now they had a special model for that purpose, even though it was really just a variation of the Town Car.

Prices for the Model T were lowered again in 1915:
Touring Car: $440
Coupelet: $590
Runabout: $390
Town Car: $640

One of the most popular Model T Fords over the past thirty years has been the Roadster/Runabout, like the 1915 example shown here.

Bob Langworthy owns this nice-looking 1915 Model T Pie Wagon.

In other Ford-related news this year, the Henry Ford Hospital was opened in Detroit, and Ford purchased 2,000 acres of prime land along the banks of the Rouge River, where groundbreaking began for a new, larger assembly plant.

Henry Ford was now constantly approached by all sorts of people to support a myriad of causes. One of those groups was a pacifist organization that wanted Ford to bankroll its efforts to stop the war being waged in Europe. These people convinced Ford that a man of his stature could help them bring World War I to a fast ending. Ford made arrangements to sail with them to Europe to bring their message of peace to all the European capitals. In December 1915, they boarded a ship called the *Oscar II* and set sail for Eu-

A Model T Ford Roadster with a pickup body conversion makes for a sporty-looking light duty truck.

The same chassis was also popular with other truck body equipment manufacturers who built bodies like this "Red Crown Gasoline" unit. Note also that this Model T conversion features a chain drive system powering the rear end.

The Model T chassis was popular with fire fighting equipment manufacturers who liked them because they were cheap to buy and their strength allowed them to carry a lot of weight without fear of breakage.

Model T Taxicabs, like this 1915 model shown here, have always been rare cars, even when they were new. This one wears a unique, homemade front bumper.

They don't get much plainer than this all black 1917 Model T Touring Car.

rope. Halfway across the Atlantic Ocean, Ford caught a bad cold and started to grow weary of the peace initiative. Upon docking, Ford bid the entourage farewell and good luck and returned to the United States. The peace initiative failed and the war raged on for another two years. Henry Ford reversed his position and put his support behind our war efforts when the United States was dragged into the action in 1917. He even offered to donate all his war profits to the US Treasury at the end of the war, but as far as anyone knows he never followed through on this promise. Nevertheless, he was still a folk hero to millions of Americans.

For 1916, Ford made some more changes to his beloved Model T, the most pronounced of which involved replacing the old brass radiator with a taller, thinner, more rounded design. Ford also painted these radiators body color, so the Model T's front end was now devoid of any significant brightness. By changing the radiator, Ford also had to change the hood line, making it taller so that it would match the radiator height. Other 1916 changes involved changing the aluminum hood to one of steel and dropping brass plating from all parts and trim.

Changes were kept to a minimum in 1917, but that didn't mean that Henry Ford didn't have any new offerings to showcase this year. Ford had much to boast of this year, especially in the commercial and farm markets. In the commercial marketplace, Ford introduced a one-ton truck and a stripped-down one-ton chassis. This news was well received by the business community because now they could buy a Ford truck instead of relying on a car conversion to meet their needs.

After years of experimenting and devel-

Model T Roadsters don't come much cuter than this one. Note the side mounted tool box and spare tire.

This magazine ad from February of 1916 shows that there were lots of accessories offered to the Model T Ford owner. *Jerry Bougher Ads*

opment work, Ford released its new Fordson tractor. It was no secret that Ford hated the drudgery of farmwork. As a matter of fact, this was the motivating force that caused him to seek his fortune in the city. He was delighted now that he finally had a reliable mechanical "workhorse." On July 27, 1917, he and his son Edsel announced the formation of a new company, "Henry Ford and Son," to produce tractors. Production at this new company started slowly, with only about 250 tractors, but within a year, those production numbers topped the 6,000 unit mark. Many went to England to help out in their war efforts.

Before we leave 1917 there is one more bit of news that we should mention since it would have a profound affect on the future of the Ford Motor Company. That news was the birth of a son to Edsel and Eleanor Ford, and he was named Henry Ford II in honor of his grandfather. A quarter of a century later, this son would have to wrestle his grandfather for control of the company that bore their names.

As in the previous model year, few changes were implemented in 1918. One change, though, involved the dropping of the unpopular Coupelet.

At the Rouge River assembly plant, Ford workers were building Eagle boats for the war

A young couple out for a Sunday drive in a muddied Model T Roadster. The chains on the rear wheels are a commentary on road conditions at that time. *Ken Halvorsen Collection*

Detailed look at the front end of an early model Model T. Note brass radiator, radiator cap, and headlamps.

effort. The first one was launched on July 11 and immediately pressed into service. A steady stream of them followed until the armistice was signed four months later. In addition to building Eagle boats, Henry Ford contributed to the war effort by sending quite a few Model Ts to Europe, several of which saw service as ambulances and received high praise for being able to go anywhere and do anything required to get the job done.

Bowing to popular demand in Michigan, Henry Ford agreed to run for a state Senate seat. Unfortunately, he lost this race by about 7,500 votes to Truman Newberry, a former Secretary of the Navy.

Edsel Ford was elected president of the Ford Motor Company on December 31, 1918, when Henry Ford "retired." Edsel's name might have been on the door, but everyone knew that Henry still controlled the company—and it would stay that way for a number of years.

Another "Brass Era" Roadster sits proudly on display at a Model T Ford show in the 1990s.

Simplicity in form and function is what we see in this Model T Speedster. Note the three pedals on floorboard, the shifter for auxiliary transmission, the coil box, and the monocle windshield clamp strapped to the steering column.

Another view of an early Model T front end. Note brass plated radiator shell, headlamps, and horn. This white painted car also uses a plated hood.

Branches

With demand growing for the Model T by leaps and bounds every year, Henry Ford and his managers needed to set up a system by which they could control marketing and distribution. Thus was born the concept of Branch offices. The following cities were designated as Ford Motor Company Branch Offices in 1913:

Atlanta, GA; Boston, MA; Buffalo, NY; Calgary, Alberta, Canada; Cambridge, MA; Charlotte, NC; Chicago, IL; Cincinnati, OH; Cleveland, OH; Columbus, OH; Dallas, TX; Denver, CO; Detroit, MI; Fargo, ND; Hamburg, Germany; Hamilton, Ontario, Canada; Houston, TX; Indianapolis, IN; Kansas City, MO; London, England; London, Ontario, Canada; Long Island City, NY; Los Angeles, CA; Louisville, KY; Manchester, England; Melbourne, Australia; Memphis, TN; Minneapolis, MN; Montreal, Quebec, Canada; New York, NY; Oklahoma City, OK; Omaha, NE; Paris, France; Philadelphia, PA; Pittsburgh, PA; Portland, OR; St. Louis, MO; St. Paul, MN; San Francisco, CA; Saskatoon, Saskatchewan, Canada; Seattle, WA; Toronto, Ontario, Canada; Vancouver, British Columbia, Canada; Walkerville, Ontario, Canada; and Winnipeg, Manitoba, Canada.

Shock absorbers, or snubbers, had to be the most popular of all the aftermarket parts for the Model T, judging by the large number of ads for this type of product. *Carl King Ads*

American-LaFrance was one of the manufacturers who produced fire fighting equipment for the Model T Ford. This ad, which appeared in the *Saturday Evening Post*, was meant to appeal to Ford dealers as well as to town councils. *Carl King Ads*

Chapter 4

1919-1920: Closing Out a Very Busy Decade

★★★ 1919-1920 Model T Coupe
★★★★1/2 1919-1920 Model T Town Car
★★★1/2 1919-1920 Model T Center Door Sedan
★★★★ 1919-1920 Model T Runabout/Roadster
★★★★ 1919-1920 Model T Touring Car

The big news for the Model T this year was the availability of an optional 6v self-starting system for closed models. It was not as reliable as the system we take for granted—in cold weather after three or four tries, one had to revert back to the old manual or "armstrong" method—but seventy-five years ago, this was a giant leap forward in the automotive world.

As much as we glamorize those days of old for their simplicity of life, hand-cranking an automobile, especially in cold weather, was a hard job and not a pleasant experience. For some reason, Ford offered this option in 1919 but only on his closed models at first. Why he didn't offer it straight across the board is a matter of speculation at this point. One of the reasons

A large supply of "vintage tin" can be found at "Easy Jacks Auto Parts" near Junction City, Kansas. This part of the salvage yard is full of Model T parts.

A Model T fire engine appearing in the 1994 Denver St. Patrick's Day Parade.

This colorful Model T Calliope Truck is a popular attraction wherever it goes.

might have had something to do with the fact that open cars far outsold closed models in the Model T line, and Henry Ford might have seen this as an opportunity to sell more closed cars. Cars equipped with this self-starting system featured a ring gear on the flywheel which meshed with a starter gear to get everything moving, as well as different timing gears and timing gear covers and modified transmission covers to mount the starter. All model T engines and transmissions featured these changes by the end of the model year.

Another option Ford offered on closed cars this year was a demountable rim that could be easily removed and replaced with a spare. Back in those days, getting a flat tire on an automobile trip was a pretty common occurrence. Before demountable rims, drivers had to fix the tires on the spot—not an easy task. Plenty of trips were ruined when time had to be taken to repair a tire to get back to town. But with a demountable rim, drivers could remove a flat tire, replace it with a spare, and fix the tire back in town.

Ford decided to branch out this year into non-automotive businesses. One such venture

Close-up view of a Model T wooden spoke wheel. Note Ford script on hub-cap.

This Model T Touring Car has a custom-made hood and radiator cover. Also note accessory oil, water, and gasoline cans carried on the runningboard.

White painted wire wheels add a sporty touch to this all black Model T Touring Car.

Now here is a gent who really knows how to make a Model T Ford earn its keep. Can't say for sure which model year this Model T is but when this photo was taken it had been converted into a pickup truck.

was the formation of his own newspaper, the *Dearborn Independent*. Henry Ford figured that since this was his newspaper and he was a folk hero, he could say just about anything he pleased. Some of his editorials, especially the ones in which he lashed out at Jewish people, would come back to haunt him in the years to come. Other news on the worldwide Ford front this year included the opening of a new assembly plant in Copenhagen, Denmark. Sales and demand for Ford's Universal Car were still growing, especially in Europe, and this new Danish plant would help Ford meet some of that demand. An autocrat who wanted to run his company his own way, Henry Ford disliked bankers and stockbrokers—and his intrusive partners. With sales of his Model T growing every year, Ford was earning quite a large fortune in profits, but he still wasn't satisfied. He wanted 100% control of the company and in 1919 he saw his chance to get it by purchasing as much stock as possible without borrowing. Instead, Ford coerced and manipulated his bankers, stockbrokers, dealers,

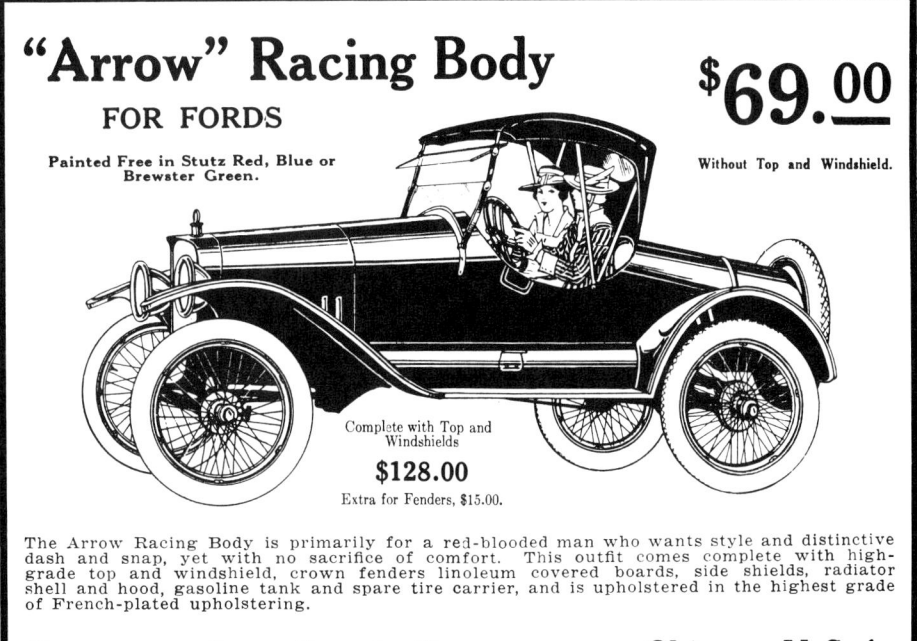

These two ads appeared in the July 1919 issue of the *Fordowner* magazine. *Jerry Bougher Ads*

A four-speed auxiliary transmission for the Model T Ford was quite an advancement over its stock, planetary type, two-speed unit. *Jerry Bougher Ads*

agents, suppliers, and customers into paying him the money he needed to buy everyone out; when he couldn't force people to sell, he threatened to leave the company and start a new one with his son Edsel. This ploy worked, and Ford got everything he was after. This deal is said to have cost Ford $105,000,000, but he probably figured the deal was worth it because now he could run the company the way he wanted without any outside interference and all of the company was controlled by the Ford family. This one-sidedness would be both a blessing and a curse to the Ford Motor Company in the future. The Ford family would call all the shots for the company now and would continue to do so even after Henry Ford II took the company back to the stock market in 1956.

The 1920 Model Ts looked pretty much the way they did in earlier model years, but three changes made them more appealing to a wider audience. The self-starter option was now available on any Model T for an additional $75; in 1920 dollars, this was a lot of money, and quite a few people ordered their Model Ts without this feature in 1920. Another option available for all Model Ts this year was the demountable rim, which retailed for $21.

The third change involved redesigning the gasoline tank from a round shape to a shorter oval in anticipation of plans to shorten the height of the Model T body so that it would look more modern. Remember that the Model T's gasoline tank was carried under the driver's seat at this time, and it was very important that the driver's seat didn't sit too high in relation to the body in any redesign. So going to a shorter tank allowed both the seat and body to maintain a proper relationship.

Employees at Ford's Highland Park assembly plant were building Model Ts as fast as they could now—so fast in fact that they were running out of storage room at the plant. On March 27, 1920, they set a new daily production record of 4,256 Model Ts during one 24hr

A Model T Touring Car with some side curtains in place sits next to a Closed Cab Model T Truck in this photograph taken at a Model T Meet.

period. Henry Ford and his workers were definitely putting America on wheels now.

In still more related news this year, Henry Ford purchased some large tracts of timberland on Michigan's Upper Peninsula in an area called Iron Mountain. There, he built a town and a large sawmill to shape raw materials into parts needed for his growing automotive empire.

Ford also went to Kentucky and West Virginia to buy some coal mines to supply raw materials for his plants, and to get that coal from the mines to his plants he bought the Detroit, Toledo, and Ironton Railroad, paying $5,000,000 initially and millions more to keep it running over the years. In addition to the railroad, Ford bought and maintained a fleet of freighters to haul raw materials to his plants and cars away from those same plants. In one decade, Ford rose from a local power in Michigan to a world power who had no equal in 1920.

Henry Ford liked to promote the fact that his Model T Fords were tough enough to go anywhere their owners wanted them to, as depicted in this magazine ad. *Carl King Ads*

During the late 'teens, a number of manufacturers made conversion units for turning Model T Roadsters into pickup trucks. As this ad shows, this Duplex unit retailed for $57.50 (F.O.B. Detroit). *Jerry Bougher Ads*

Chapter 5

1921: A New Decade and Some New Direction

★★★1/2	1921-1922 Model T Coupe
★★★★	1921-1922 Model T Runabout/Roadster
★★★★	1921-1922 Model T Touring Car
★★★1/2	1921-1922 Model T Center Door Sedan
★★★★	1921-1922 Model T Sportster
★★	1921-1922 Model T Commercial
★★	1921-1922 Model TT Trucks

For 1921, the Model T stayed pretty much the same and changes were kept to a minimum. To boost sales and recoup some of the money the company lost in 1920 and to recover some of the costs incurred with his company takeover in 1919, Henry Ford dropped prices

Archie Lewis, of Albuquerque, New Mexico, owns this beautiful Model T Ford "Huckster" Wagon which he restored some time ago. Trucks like these are a rare sight today, but sixty or seventy years ago they were pretty common on streets all over America.

This unrestored Model T Ford Sedan is a popular attraction at car shows in the southwest.

Most Model T trucks of the early 1920s, like the one shown here, used wooden cabs and bodies.

again this year. For example, the Model T Coupe, which returned to the lineup in 1919, cost $695 in 1920 but $595 the next year, and the $370 Runabout was now available for $325. Several customers were drawn to Ford showrooms this year to take advantage of Ford's lower prices. Production in turn jumped more than 40,000 units to a new high mark of 989,785.

Henry Ford admired an automotive pioneer by the name of Henry Leland, who had been involved in the first car company that Ford started back at the turn of the century. This company would later become the Cadillac Motor Company, and Leland was the man who helped that company reach a plateau where it became the "Standard of the World." Leland's primary claim to fame in the automotive world was the standardization of automotive parts. Prior to Leland's standards, the business of making cars was basically a hodge-podge affair of entrepreneurs each doing his own thing. No two parts were exactly alike, and quality and durability suffered.

In the 1920s, Bell Telephone linemen used trucks like this when they were installing telephone services in communities from border to border, and coast to coast.

A restored 1922 Model TT truck at a Florida car show in 1991. Model TT trucks are starting to show up at car and truck shows throughout the country. Elliott Kahn Photo

Here is an example of a Model T truck with an aftermarket cab and pickup truck body.

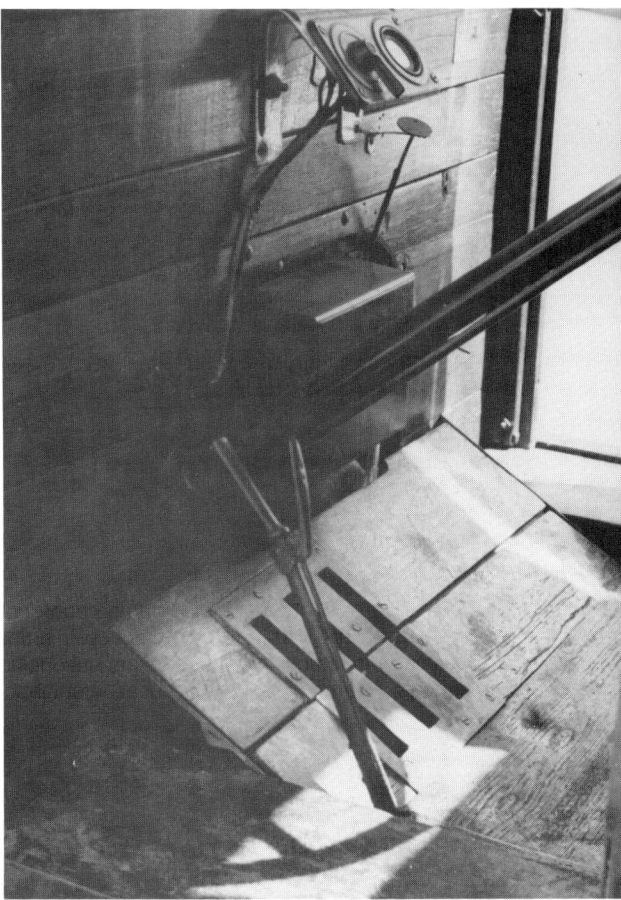

Model T truck cabs were pretty stark as compared with Ford trucks of later eras. Note the three slots in the floor for the three pedals that once used to shift the Model T and apply its brakes. Along with an emergency brake handle, a choke cable, ignition switch, gauges, steering column, steering wheel, and a seat, this was about all a Model T Ford truck owner could get from the factory.

When Leland showed people that they could set standards and stick with them, the auto business would be in better shape, and when the time came to replace broken or worn out parts, exact duplicates were available. Without Leland's standards, the automobile business wouldn't have made the giant steps in its progression in such a short time. In only ten years, we had gone from the experimental stage of a motorized buggy to a dependable four-wheeled, reasonably comfortable vehicle.

Leland soon tired of politics at Cadillac and started his own company, the Lincoln Motor Company, to build Liberty aircraft engines for the US government during World War I. Leland's company did very well during the war, but when he began producing automobiles, he was hit hard by the postwar Depression. Leland's cars were called Lincolns and they were cars of uncompromising quality, but few could afford them. Without strong sales to fill the company coffers, Leland soon found himself in dire financial straits. He needed to find a partner and turned to Ford, who had the capital to invest and agreed to buy out the assets of the Lincoln Motor Company if Leland would stay on and run it. Leland agreed to these terms, and so on February 4, 1921, he and Ford, along with their sons Wilfred and Edsel, signed a historic document transferring the company over to the Fords.

The Leland-Ford connection turned out to be a shaky one at best and within a year or so, the Lelands, tired of fighting with Henry Ford, left the company in a huff. The addition of the Lincoln to the Ford Motor Company added a bit of prestige to the company just when it needed it the most. Now Ford had a low-priced car at one end of the market and a high-priced, premiere vehicle at the other end of the spectrum.

This is what a well-stocked Ford agency looked like back in the 1920s. Notice that this dealer, probably located in a small farming town, also handled Fordson tractors.

There weren't any changes of note to report for the 1922 Model Ts and Lincolns, but other corporate-level changes would have an effect on the company for many years to come. Ford opened two new plants in Antwerp, Belgium and Trieste, Italy, to cater to the increased demand for Model Ts in Europe. Model T production totals passed the 1.2 million mark by the end of the model year.

That was the good news. But along with good news, there sometimes is bad news, and the bad news this year concerned a man by the name of William S. Knudsen. Henry Ford was a good automobile man who deserves all the credit he has received, but the success of the Ford Motor Company and its products was definitely not a one-man show. Many talented individuals helped Ford reach this position of fame and fortune. Knudsen was one of these individuals.

Knudsen was probably partly responsible for refining the Model T to make it more appealing to the American marketplace. In 1921, Knudsen was reportedly second in command at Ford. Although this position was a valuable one, Knudsen thought he deserved more power and that Ford didn't appreciate him enough, even though Ford put him on a pedestal with several underlings to order around.

Although Knudsen didn't realize it at the time, the only position above him at Ford was Henry Ford's seat and as far as Henry Ford was concerned, only a person by the name of Ford would sit in that seat. A disgruntled Knudsen let it be known that he wasn't pleased with that attitude and in a move that shocked Henry Ford and the Detroit automotive community, left Ford and became Chevrolet's general manager in 1922.

Ford considered this move a stab in the heart because Chevrolet was his chief rival. Knudsen's main goal at Chevrolet was to catch up to and eventually surpass Ford as the world's largest automaker. It took him about five years to reach this goal, but when the Model T went out of production in 1927, Knudsen was there with his Chevrolets. For the first time, Chevrolet and Knudsen beat Ford at his own game and both have never looked back—Ford, for the most part, remaining in Chevrolet's shadow ever since.

Note on the sign above the door of this garage the mechanic or proprietor of this garage lists himself as a "Ford Doctor." That's one of his Model T patients coming out of the door.

This Model T Ford is equipped with a leather strap to hold its crank handle in place. The cow bell strapped to the front axle suggests that this is a rural Model T.

A couple of beautiful Model T Roadsters sit side by side getting ready to enter another tour.

The "Smith-Form-A-Truck" was the grandfather of all Model T truck conversions. Their kits included pieces to extend and strengthen the frame, and relocate the rear axle.

Chapter 6

1923: A New Look for a Grand Old Lady

★★★1/2	1923-1924 Model T Coupe
★★★★	1923-1924 Model T Runabout/Roadster
★★★★	1923-1924 Model T Touring Car
★★★	1923-1924 Model T Two Door Sedan
★★★	1923-1924 Model T Four Door Sedan
★★★1/2	1923-1924 Model T Roadster Pickup Truck
★★★★	1923-1924 Model T Sportster
★★★	1923-1924 Model T Commercial
★★	1923-1924 Model TT Truck

For the first time since 1917, a redesigned body, lowered to give a more streamlined appearance, appeared on the Model T frame in 1923. These Model Ts also featured a taller radiator that now sported an apron at its lower end.

The Center Door Sedan was replaced by two new sedan models: the four-door model called the Fordor Sedan and the two-door Tudor Sedan. Both featured crank-up glass windows in their doors, a first for Ford. The

A group of Model T Ford owners gathered together to put their cars on display at a California car show a couple of years ago. Both Model T and Model A Fords are popular in California and it's not uncommon to see groups of them together on a pretty regular basis.

Ford introduced the Station Wagon in 1929. Before that, if anyone was in need of such a vehicle the only recourse was to purchase an aftermarket Depot Hack body to mount on a Model T chassis. Dan Olsen, of Quakertown, PA, owns this beautiful example of a Model T Depot Hack. *Dan Olsen photo*

A few Model T Roadsters like the 1923 model shown here were converted into pickups by removing the "turtle deck" rear end and mounting a pickup box in its place. *Don Bunn photo*

Coupe now featured an integral trunk area as part of its body, while the Roadster still relied on a separate body and "turtle back" arrangement.

The Touring Car featured a new "one-man" fabric top that did away with some of the support braces needed earlier. These cars, along with the Roadster, also featured a new raked windshield frame, which added a sporty flair to their designs. All 1923 Model Ts also featured a new cowl ventilator door that provided a little more airflow into the interior.

In July 1923, a new milestone was set when the "Eight Millionth" Model T came down the assembly line. This was a mark nobody ever expected these cars to hit, but even so, Ford sensed that sales were starting to slip. He decided to help bolster sales by initiating a very heavy direct mail campaign and by implementing a savings plan whereby customers could set aside a certain amount of money each week to put towards the purchase of a new Ford. This program was officially dubbed the "Ford Weekly Purchase Plan."

Both plans were successful, and a new production level was set by the end of the model year. In 1923, a total of 2,055,309 Ford vehicles left Ford assembly lines, boosting company profits to $82 million.

The 1924 Model T looked pretty much the same as it did in 1923.

Even though Ford opened new overseas plants this year in Chile, Sweden, and South Africa, Model T production actually slipped this year.

A second record was set in June 1923 when the "Ten Millionth" Ford rolled off the assembly line at the Highland Park plant. This milestone car, a Touring Car with a "10,000,000th" logo emblazoned on its sides, was driven on a cross-country promotional tour by Frank Kulick—the same man who drove one of the original Ford race cars in the 1909 transcontinental race. Millions of people saw this "Ten Millionth" Ford as it traveled through many cities and towns on its way across the United States.

Ford lowered prices again this year, and a new low mark was reached with the 1924 Runabout going for an unbelievable $265. A good used Model T could be had for $50 to $75, and one needing some work could cost $20 or less. Be that as it may, at the end of the 1924 model year, even though he sold fewer cars, Henry Ford made more money. His profits in 1924 totaled about $100,000,000.

The Ford Motor Company reached a milestone with the production of the "Ten Millionth" Model T, a Touring Car, during 1924. This Ford publicity photo shows Henry Ford with the milestone car and his first Ford, called a "Quadricycle." *Ford Motor Company*

This Model TT Ford truck is owned by Morgan Trucking of Muscatine, Iowa. *Don Bunn photo*

"Fill her up," the driver seems to be saying to the gas jockey in this photo. The model shown is a Model T Coupe.

A couple of young women get ready to take a spin in their new Model T Coupe. This was a fashionable car for young ladies in those days.

Here is a sporty-looking Model T racer. On the back end of the car is a 1922 California license tag. Note the bucket seats, oval gas tank, and a header exhaust pipe coming out of the hood.

A front end view of the same Model T racer. Note fuel priming pump mounted on the cowl and a nose snubbing devil radiator ornament.

These Model T Fords gathered together in Albuquerque, New Mexico in 1992 on what was called the "Over The Hill Tour." This name refers to their drive up into the Sandia Mountains on Albuquerque's eastern side.

This is a 1923 Model T Ford Roadster Pickup. It is equipped with wind wings, Moto-Meter radiator cap, and it also has a tarp mounted on top of its body to protect its cargo.

This Model T Touring Car from Kansas is equipped with a few vintage accessories from that era, including a Boyce "Moto-Meter" radiator cap, cowl lamps, a runningboard-mounted toolbox, and a hand-operated turn signal arm.

The Model T Fordor Sedan, like the one shown here, was one of the most popular and best-selling Model Ts of the 1920s.

Another Model T Coupe, this one a 1926 model, sits out on display at a car show surrounded by some more modern vehicles.

This Model T Sedan, sitting at a car show in the 1970s is a hot rod which has been treated to an engine swap, custom wheels and tires, and a colorful paint job.

A lineup of beautiful, restored Model T Fords await their turn under the scrutinizing eyes of the judges at a car show.

This Model T engine has been modified for some extra power by the use of a Frontenac overhead valve conversion head. The popular Frontenac head was designed and manufactured by the Chevrolet brothers for use on the Model T engines of the time.

A Model T Roadster sits on display amid some other collectible Fords at a car show in the mid-eighties in Albuquerque, New Mexico.

This shot of a Model T Touring Car shows how the rear window was treated on these tops. The rear window canvas panel could be unsnapped to give a much larger view.

The Ten-Millionth

The 10,000,000th Ford car left the Highland Park factories of the Ford Motor Company June 4. This is a production achievement unapproached in automotive history. Tremendous volume has been the outgrowth of dependable, convenient, economical service.

Ford Motor Company
Detroit, Michigan

Runabout $265   Coupe $525   Tudor Sedan $590   Fordor Sedan $685
All prices f. o. b. Detroit

The Touring Car
$295
F. O. B. Detroit
Demountable Rims and Starter $85 extra

As you can well imagine, the "Ten-Millionth" Model T was something to publicize, and Ford took advantage of the opportunity.

Chapter 7

1925: The Beginning of the End for Henry's Lizzie

★★★★	1925-1927 Model T Roadster/Runabout
★★★★1/2	1925-1927 Model T Touring Car
★★★1/2	1925-1927 Model T Coupe
★★★	1925-1927 Model T Two Door Sedan
★★★	1925-1927 Model T Four Door Sedan
★★★1/2	1925-1927 Model T Roadster Pickup Truck
★★★	1925-1927 Model T Commercial
★★	1925-1927 Model TT Truck
★★★★	1925-1927 Model T Speedster

By the time 1925 rolled around, everyone but Henry Ford was convinced that the days of the Model T Ford were numbered. They realized that no matter what he did to make the car look more appealing, the competition had caught up and was nibbling at Ford's lead. Deceptively, the Model T was still the number one seller, but its customers were starting to demand more of their cars and the Model T was beginning to look more like an alternate choice.

Once again, Ford lowered prices on his Model Ts to help stimulate sales. These price reductions ranged from $5 for a new Runabout to $25 on a Fordor Sedan.

1925 Model T Prices
Touring Car: $290
Runabout: $260
Coupe: $520
Tudor Sedan: $580
Fordor Sedan: $660

Two new options this year included balloon tires and a manual windshield wiper. The price of the wiper isn't known, but the balloon tire option cost about $25. These tires measured 4.40x21x30in, compared to the 3.5x30in standard clincher type. Model Ts equipped with these tires sat a little bit higher than Model Ts using clincher tires, and their ride was a little bit softer.

A new offering from Ford this year would put Ford firmly in the driver's seat of the light commercial vehicle market. In April 1925, Ford introduced its first factory-produced pickup, the Ford Model T Runabout with Pickup Truck Body. It retailed for $281 and was an immediate hit with commercial

This Model TT Closed Cab Truck from about 1925 has been fitted with an aftermarket dump body. *Don Bunn photo*

51

This 1926 Model T Fordor Sedan features cowl lamps from an earlier model. In 1926 this version was the most popular Model T in the Ford lineup.

A nickel-plated radiator shell was a new feature found on the Model T Fords beginning in 1926, and it added some much-needed sparkle to Henry's "Universal Car."

Another 1926 Model T Touring Car. This car looks a lot sportier equipped with wire wheels instead of wheels with wood spokes.

car buyers. In just this model year alone, Ford produced almost 34,000 of them. At about this same time, Ford announced the addition of an all-steel closed cab for its larger Model TT trucks.

Ford opened new plants this year in Japan, Australia, and Mexico, and its British plant celebrated a milestone with the production of its 250,000th Model T.

Ford's "all-black" policy became a thing of the past in 1926 when Ford once again started offering blue, gray, and brown exterior color choices in addition to black for its closed car models. Color choices weren't the only changes seen on these new Fords in 1926. In all Model Ts except the Fordor Sedan, the gas tanks were moved under the cowl area and fuel filled through the ventilator door; the Fordor Sedan still carried its fuel tank under the driver's seat. All Model Ts this year had wider running boards and came with 4.40x21in balloon tires as standard equipment. Wooden spoke wheels were still standard fare, but wire wheels were available at an extra cost.

Runabout models now featured an integral rear deck like that on the Coupe model introduced in 1923, and the Touring Car joined

Though Ford was offering a pickup box by 1926, some people still preferred to buy a chassis and install their own body, like this one installed on this 1926 chassis. *Elliott Kahn photo*

"Speedsters" are fun vehicles to drive as evidenced by the smile on this driver's face.

chassis, which made them look sportier than their predecessors. Closed cars got a new one-piece windshield, and fenders were re-designed on all cars. Both the hood and the bodies on the 1926 Model T were longer than those used on the 1925 versions. More louvers were punched into the 1926 hood to help aid cooling, and spare tires were carried on a bracket mounted on the rear of most Model Ts.

Bowing to safety concerns, Ford fixed some larger brake drums on the rear of all Model Ts built this year. The Model T wasn't known for its braking prowess, but at least these new models stopped better than the older ones.

All cars featured a new nickel-plated radiator shell and headlight rings. At the beginning of the model year, the headlights on all Model Ts were carried on two separate stands, but after January 1, 1926, they were mounted on a bar across the front of the car to join the two front fenders. This bar also added a little torsional rigidity to the front end of the Model T.

its Canadian-built cousins by boasting a functional driver's door this year.

These Model Ts also sat on a lowered

The fire chief who originally drove this Model T Roadster must have been a sporting fellow judging by the white wall tires, red spoke wheels, and lots of bells and whistles.

Some of the fastest Model T racers back in the 1920s and 1930s were the "Fronty-Fords" so named because they ran Frontenac overhead valve heads, which in some cases doubled or tripled their horsepower outputs. Shown here is a restored "Fronty Ford" that raced as the "Bob Estes Special."

This Model T Coupe features a commercial box-type body in place of its "turtle deck" rear end. Though you probably can't see the writing on the box it says "Coca Cola Sales and Service," indicating that this Model T was probably a route salesman's car.

Sometime during the 1926 model year, Henry Ford finally realized that the time had come to put his beloved T out to pasture, so he instructed his engineers to begin working on the Model T's successor.

Few changes were made or contemplated for the 1927 model year, the last year for the Model T. Wire wheels became standard and wooden spoke wheels became optional, and color choices included blue, black, brown, gray, green, or maroon. Another milestone was reached at Highland Park on May 26, 1927, when the 15,000,000th Model T came off the assembly line to thunderous applause. Less than one month later, the last Model T left that same assembly line and the plant was closed down. This plant would reopen seven months later to produce some of the Model As that would debut on December 2, 1927. While the plant was shut down, some of its assembly line equipment was moved to the Fordson Plant down on the banks of the Rouge River, where Ford was starting to build the largest industrial complex the world had ever known.

The official number of Model Ts built during this nineteen-year period stood at 15,007,033, a mark that wouldn't be bested until the Volkswagen Beetle did it forty years later. Some say this was Ford's finest hour.

In the twenties, if you weren't satisfied with the body that your Ford came with you could buy a replacement body through the aftermarket. *Jerry Bougher Ads*

Camping in a car or truck isn't a new recreational activity by any stretch of the imagination. Here we see a conversion kit that was offered to Model T owners back in the early twenties. This conversion kit turned your Model T into a "comfortable home on wheels." *Jerry Bougher Ads*

Highlights at the Highland Park Plant

- The home of the Model T.
- Automotive mass production by means of a moveable assembly line introduced at this plant (Which plant is this?) in 1913.
- At one time, the largest building of its kind under one roof.
- Main building at this complex was four stories high, 865ft long, and 75ft wide.
- Building contained 50,000sq-ft of glass in its windows to let in natural light.
- Complex built on a 130-acre site.
- Bounded by Woodward Avenue, Manchester, Oakland, and Ferris Streets in the Highland Park section of Detroit.
- Plant put into production in 1910.
- At one time, the largest automobile assembly plant in the world.
- Plant designed by noted industrial designer Albert Kahn.
- In addition to the assembly plant, a large foundry was built on the site. Other buildings located at this complex were a power plant and a large machine shop.
- Machine shop alone was 840ft long and 140ft wide.
- The plant was opened for visitor tours for quite some time. In 1925 alone, more than 156,000 people toured the plant.
- Peak employment at the plant was reached in 1925 when the yearly payroll covered more than 68,000 employees.
- A $5 per day wage was introduced at this plant.
- In addition to Model Ts, industrial engines, tractors, and other Ford cars and trucks were built at this plant.
- The plant was closed in 1974.
- The plant was demolished by developers in the mid-1970s.

Here's a new Model T Fordor Sedan in 1926.

Racing to a Tee

Although they weren't originally designed to be racing cars, quite a few Model Ts were modified and entered in competitive events all over the country.

Thousands of backyard mechanics and drivers wanted to go racing but couldn't afford to buy a racing car. They could afford to buy a used Model T for $20, however, and spend another few hundred dollars for some hop-up equipment. These cars couldn't win the Indy 500, but they could run fast and win at their local dirt track—and some of the best drivers did manage to move up in the ranks to race at Indianapolis.

A winning Model T racer required a more powerful engine, one that put out at least twice the stock output of 20hp. The easiest way to build a more powerful engine was to replace the head, intake manifold, carburetor, magneto, and exhaust manifold with performance-boosting parts offered by such aftermarket suppliers as Winfield, Zenith, Bosch, Rajo, Warfield, and Frontenac.

Of all the parts available, nothing produced more power from the Model T engine than an overhead valve conversion head from the likes of Rajo, Craig-Hunt, Riley, Roof, Winfield, and Frontenac. The most famous of these heads were from Frontenac, a brand name for heads manufactured by the Chevrolet brothers. Fords equipped with these heads were called Fronty-Fords.

Some Fronty-Fords found their way to Indianapolis, where they ran against the Duesenbergs, Millers, Talbots, and other pure racing machines. One year, a Fronty-Ford even managed to finish an Indy 500 race in fifth position, not too bad a performance from a car that was basically a backyard special. These Fronty-Fords were probably the precursors to the hot rods that would follow in the next decade or so.

In the 1920s, the Chevrolet brothers offered more than one type of Frontenac head for the Model T, ranging from the Model "T" head for touring use to the "SR" and "D-O" heads for racing. The "D-O" stood for chain-driven dual overhead cams. These heads also featured four valves per cylinder, relocated spark plugs, and a host of other "go-fast" goodies. In racing form, they boosted the Model T's engine output from 20hp to more than 80hp—and 80hp in a car as light as a stripped-down Model T could make such a car fly.

Building and supplying Frontenac heads to Model T racers turned out to be a lucrative business for the Chevrolet brothers. During the 1920s, they sold more than 10,000 of them. That is probably why these heads are so easy to find today and make a nice addition to any Model T.-

The nickel-plated radiator shell and wire wheels identify this Model T Tudor Sedan as a 1926 or 1927 model.

A fully restored Model T Roadster on display at a car show in the 1990s. White wire spoke wheels and white tire cover add a sporty look to this particular car.

Model T Roadsters are popular with restorers and a number of them can always be seen at car shows from coast to coast.

Whitewall tires really brighten up the looks of this Model T Tudor Sedan. This car also makes for an eye-catching rolling political billboard.

The ultimate 1950s hot rod. A black Model T Roadster with a wild flame job, wide whitewalls, and a hopped-up Flathead Ford engine for motivation.

$520 F.O.B. Detroit was a good price to pay for a Model T Coupe in the mid-twenties. *Carl King Ads*

Easier to handle– safer to drive

The driving control of the Ford car is exceedingly simple, yet always dependable. It effectively reduces the possibilities of accidents—particularly in crowded city traffic. Foot pedal gear changing, powerful brakes, short wheelbase and full visibility, afforded by the all-steel body construction with narrower pillars and large plate-glass windows, are important reasons why Ford owners enjoy such security. Let the nearest Authorized Ford Dealer explain the many features of Ford cars and demonstrate their easy handling. Get full particulars about convenient time payment plans.

RUNABOUT, $260 · TOURING, $290 · COUPE, $520
TUDOR SEDAN, $580 · FORDOR SEDAN, $660
Closed cars in colors. · Demountable rims and starter extra on open cars. *All prices F. O. B. Detroit*

FORD MOTOR COMPANY, DETROIT, MICH.

"Easier to handle–safer to drive." This ad lists all the attributes that a Model T has over the competition in handling and safety aspects. *Carl King Ads*

Chapter 8

Henry Makes a Lady out of Lizzie

★★★★★	1928 Model A Four Door Phaeton
★★★★1/2	1928 Model A Roadster
★★★	1928 Model A Coupe
★★★1/2	1928 Model A Sport Coupe
★★★	1928 Model A Tudor Sedan
★★★	1928 Model A Fordor Sedan
★★★1/2	1928 Model A Roadster Pickup Truck
★★★	1928 Model A Closed Cab Pickup Truck
★★★	1928 Model A Panel Truck
★★★	1928 Model A Special Business Coupe
★★★★★	1928 Model A Town Car
★★★	1928 Model AA Truck

These days, when an auto manufacturer shuts down its plants to retool for a new model, the process usually takes three to six weeks. Such was not the case back in June 1927, when Henry Ford shut down all the Model T assembly plants to retool to produce his new and vastly improved Model As. That action closed more

A group of Model A and Model T Fords sit on display at a car show in the mid-eighties.

than thirty-six plants, put thousands of Ford workers on indefinite layoffs, and caused hundreds of Ford dealers and countless suppliers to go out of business. It also allowed Chevrolet in 1927 to catch up to Ford and surpass it in the annual sales race.

Those in the business hoped that the shutdown wouldn't last too long; even Ford Motor Company insiders thought it would take only a couple of months at best. Edsel Ford himself would make periodic announcements that the new car was just around the corner. The only one who wasn't concerned with the time frame seemed to be Henry Ford. As far as he was concerned, the Model T's successor would not be hurried in any way and people were going to have to be patient.

Henry Ford established three goals for this new car to meet. First, it had to be more stylish than the Model T. One of the chief complaints that Ford received about his Model T in the mid-1920s was that its styling now looked dated.

Second, it had to be more powerful than the Model T. Another criticism leveled against the Flivver was that the competition could run

This Model A Coupe has had its appearance brightened up by having its wheels painted a straw color. It has also been dressed up with a grille guard, wind wings, Boyce Moto-Meter radiator cap, and running-board-mounted accessory cans.

circles around it. Many people would have liked to see this new Ford get a six- or eight-cylinder engine. Ford and his engineers toyed with an X-8 engine, but it proved to be too problematic and too costly for general production in a low-priced car.

Third, the Model A would have to be easier to drive than the Model T, be more comfortable, and offer more conveniences.

These three stipulations were not very hard to comply with primarily because Ford put his best people on the project and they worked around the clock to guarantee that Ford's goals would be met. "Cast Iron" Charlie Sorensen, one of Ford's right-hand men, was put in charge of making sure that all of Ford's plants, suppliers, and anybody else remotely connected to the production of this new vehicle would be ready to go when Henry Ford gave the signal. Eugene Farkas, one of Ford's best engineers, was put in charge of the overall design of the new car. Other gifted Ford engineers worked under Farkas, including Frank Johnson (chief engineer at the Lincoln Plant), Peter Martin, and Lawrence Sheldrick. Ford left the important matter of styling up to his son Edsel and Joe Galamb, who, incidentally, worked on the Mustang project thirty-five years later. Both men had a flair for styling and this gift was reflected in the beautiful Model A, which looked like a scaled-down Lincoln.

The first Model A engine was assembled on October 20, 1927, and the first Model A prototype was driven off a pilot assembly line seven days later. By November 1, 1927, production had been upped to about twenty cars per day. These early cars were plagued by production problems, all of which had to be corrected before Henry Ford would allow any cars to be sold.

On the morning of December 1, 1927, Ford took out full-page advertisements for the Model A in 2,000 newspapers and magazines around the country. This introductory promotional campaign alone cost Ford about $2,000,000.

Official introduction day for the new Model A was December 2, 1927, and hundreds of thousands of Americans lined up to catch a glimpse of it. In a matter of days, more than 10,000,000 people got to see this car. It was one of the greatest new car introductions of all time and one of the top news stories of the day. Although Henry Ford never revealed how much he spent to develop and release the Model A, it is estimated that the total cost far exceeded $100,000,000 when everything is taken into consideration.

Quite a few Model A Fords run in the Great American Race every year. This particular car is run by a father-daughter team from Albuquerque, New Mexico.

The Model A was not only more stylish than the Model T, it debuted with a new, more powerful engine, a new transmission, four-wheel brakes, a 6v electrical system, new steel spoke wheels, and safety glass in the windshield. Other standard equipment included a windshield wiper, speedometer, fuel and oil gauges, dash light, mirror, grease gun, tool kit, bumpers, and a rear stoplight/taillight combination. Quite a bit of this equipment would have been an extra-cost option on the Model T, if it was even available.

At first, demand for the Model A far exceeded supply and by year's end, orders for the Model A had surpassed 727,000 units. Not everyone who wanted a Model A in 1928 could get one; among those lucky enough to get one were Delores Del Rio, Will Rogers, Thomas A. Edison, Lillian Gish, Cecil B. DeMille, Franklin Roosevelt, Douglas Fairbanks, and "America's Sweetheart" Mary Pickford. In fact, Douglas Fairbanks, who was a personal friend of Edsel Ford, is listed as the buyer of the first production Model A, a Sport Coupe which he presented to his wife, Mary Pickford, as a gift.

Here is a good look at a Model A four-cylinder engine. Note carburetor and intake manifold mounting.

Early 1928 Prices
Phaeton: $395
Roadster: $385
Coupe: $495
Sport Coupe with Rumble Seat: $550
Tudor Sedan: $495
Fordor Sedan: $570
Commercial Pickup Truck: $395

These new Model As featured a new L-head four-cylinder engine that displaced 200.5ci and was rated at 40hp, about twice what the Model T's 176.7ci engine put out. That higher horsepower figure translated into a higher top speed of 65mph, which was about 20mph faster than a stock Model T.

Another new feature of the Model A was a standard three-speed synchromesh sliding transmission which replaced the Model T's antiquated three-pedal planetary transmission. At first, a multiplate disc clutch was needed to hook this transmission to the engine, but beginning with the later 1928 models, a simple, single-disc setup replaced this setup.

Before the Model A, Ford didn't put four-wheel brakes on any production cars. Including four-wheel brakes as standard equipment on the Model A was overshadowed by the announcement that the Model A would be going to a six-way brake system by adding a separate system on the rear that would be con-

Wonder how many of these Model A U.S. Mail Trucks are still in existence? Don't you think it would be a kick to deliver mail in one of these trucks today?

This 1928 Model A Closed Cab Pickup has to be a late model version since the Closed Cab model wasn't offered as a pickup until after August of 1928.

Few truck buyers in 1928 ordered whitewall tires, and that's a shame, because they really dress up the look of these vehicles.

trolled by the emergency brake lever.

Like the Model T before it, the Model A featured a cowl-mounted gas tank, on the back of which was a nickel-plated gauge cluster containing a speedometer (which read to 80mph), ammeter, oil pressure gauge, and a lockable ignition switch. Spark and throttle levers were mounted on the steering column near the steering wheel, and a choke rod extended from the carburetor through the firewall to the instrument panel.

On the early cars, a red, hard rubber steering wheel was fitted with a horn button located in its center. The headlight switch was actually a ring around the horn button. On closed cars, fine cloth upholstery covered the seats, door, and side panels, whereas on open cars, leatherette was used.

Bodies for the new Model A were supplied to Ford by Murray and Briggs, two contract shops that supplied ready-made bodies

The Poco Quatros Model A Club of Albuquerque, New Mexico, always brings out a number of great-looking cars to shows.

Pictured here is a 1928 Model A Panel Truck, one of about 3,700 produced by Ford that year. *Elliott Kahn photo*

This red oxide primered Model A Tudor Sedan provides a good basic foundation for a restoration or street rod project.

This 1928 Model A Roadster features a spare tire cover, rumble seat, and whitewall tires.

to several manufacturers then. Ford also built some of its own Model A bodies that year.

Ford offered the following models in the Model A lineup in 1928: four-door Phaeton Touring Car, two-door Roadster, two-door Coupe, two-door Sport Coupe with Rumble Seat, two-door Tudor Sedan, and four-door Fordor Sedan. The company also included Commercial Cars in its early 1928 catalog. Chief among them was the Model A Pickup Truck. For the first ten months of production, this pickup was available only as an open Roadster with Pickup Truck Body because Ford was using all its Closed-Cab cabs for the heavier-duty Model AA trucks. Ford started offering the Closed-Cab Pickup Truck around August 1928. Another new addition to the Commercial Car line in August 1928 was the Panel Truck, which featured a handsome body by Budd. These trucks, or closed light-duty commercial vehicles, as they were called, featured two folding front seats, a larger cargo area, and two rear doors. They were popular with grocery stores, department stores, and other venues where an attractive delivery vehicle made a nice rolling business card.

Development on the Model A didn't stop once it was released, and changes were soon forthcoming. Front and rear bumpers were standard equipment now. On the first 200 or so cars, these were open-ended. These open-ended bumpers were replaced by bumpers whose ends curled around a metal dowel pin arrangement, which in effect made them closed-ended. Also in the middle of 1928 the emergency brake lever was moved from the driver's left side by the cowl to the center of the floor by the gearshift lever.

Another change seen on the 1928 Model A as production picked up speed was in the louver design on the sides of the hood. Early hoods featured louvers whose top line ran parallel to the bottom edge of the hood, creating a sloping effect to the design. The design was changed in the middle of the model year, so now the top edge of the louvers ran parallel to the hood hinge line. The result was a more pleasing, integrated design.

In May 1928, Henry Ford rolled out a new model meant to appeal to the businessman, the Model A Special Business Coupe. The most unique styling feature on these cars had to be their padded leather covered tops

Here is a different interpretation of a Speedster body on a Model A frame. The builder has welded two late 1940s International Harvester hoods together to form a unique rear end treatment.

Model A Roadster Pickups are popular vehicles in the world of street rodding. This red beauty has been fitted with custom wheels, big tires, and a custom fitted tarp. There is also a modern powerplant residing under the hood.

that included port hole windows. They also featured trunks and rear-mounted spare tires and retailed for $525.

Demand for the new Model A kept all of Ford's factories busy. Some dealers couldn't get enough cars and complained to Henry Ford that they weren't able to satisfy their customer's needs. They were willing to use any trick in the book to get an extra allocation of cars for their dealerships. A couple of enterprising dealers in Seattle, Washington, even took a train east to Detroit, where they presented themselves on the steps of the Highland Park plant. They told Henry Ford of their plans to revive a durability run like one that had brought the 1909 Model T transcontinental racers to him. Ford and his managers saw this as a perfect opportunity to publicly display the durability of the new Model A. So convinced were they of this project that they pulled a new Model A Sedan off the line at

In the early 1960s, a young Ken Campbell stands proudly by his first car: a 1928 Model A hot rod coupe. *Ken Campbell photo*

Highland Park and stocked it with such amenities as oil, water, extra clothes, and some food for this trek west. Thus loaded, the dealers left Dearborn and headed west on a trip that would cover more than 3,000 miles. They covered that distance in slightly fewer than 77 hours, a new record for such a trip in 1928. Upon completion, both dealers and the car were tired and dirty, but the trip was made without any major breakdowns or incidents. Ford executives were quite impressed with this accomplishment and all the good media coverage it generated.

The new Model A wasn't the only new car introduced in the low-priced field in 1928. Walter P. Chrysler released a new low-priced vehicle called the Plymouth, a stylish car that came from good stock. The Plymouth was of such good quality, in fact, that it proved to be a worthy competitor to Ford for several years.

Even though Model A sales were high this year, Chevrolet managed to sell more cars and retain the number one sales position for the second consecutive year. Even though his new Model A didn't recapture the sales lead from Chevrolet, Henry Ford couldn't have been happier with the reception his new car received in its first full model year.

The Most Popular Model A Accessory

The most popular Model A accessory in both the 1930s and now has to be the Flying Quail radiator cap. Ford sold hundreds of thousands of them, and practically every Model A one sees today has a Flying Quail sitting atop its radiator shell.

This radiator cap was originally designed by Irving R. Bacon, a Ford Motor Company artist. It originally carried part number A-18385, and its original catalog price was $3. In 1928 and 1929, these ornaments were nickel-plated castings, while the 1930-1931 versions were chrome-plated castings.

These ornaments were produced for Ford by the Stant Corporation of Connersville, Indiana. Stant also produced Motor Meter radiator caps for Ford and the Greyhounds that graced the radiator shells of Lincolns. Stant has also produced other Ford emblems and radiator caps down through the years.

The 1928 Model A engine compartment. Note the placement of the starter, generator, distributor cap, and other details.

The front end details of this early Model A Ford include a mesh radiator grille guard, Klaxon horn, Moto-Meter radiator cap, and amber-colored driving lamp.

This view of a 1928 Model A Standard Business Coupe shows rumble seat, and folding trunk carrier. Since the trunk carrier takes up room where the spare tire sits, the spare tire has been moved up to a fender well.

As you can see this is an award-winning 1928 Model A Coupe. Just count all those trophies and ribbons!

Here is another Great American Racer, this time a Model A Touring Car. Note the whitewall tires, grille guard, and headlight deflector shields.

Chapter 9

Happy Days are Here Again

1929	
★★★★1/2	1929 Model A Roadster
★★★★★	1929 Model A Phaeton
★★★★	1929 Model A Cabriolet
★★★	1929 Model A Coupe
★★★	1929 Model A Business Coupe
★★★1/2	1929 Model A Sport Coupe
★★★	1929 Model A Tudor Sedan
★★★	1929 Model A or Sedan
★★★★★	1929 Model A Town Car
★★★★	1929 Model A Station Wagon
★★★★	1929 Model A Taxi Cab
★★★1/2	1929 Model A Town Sedan
★★★	1929 Model A Special Coupe
★★★1/2	1929 Model A Fordor Sedan Delivery
★★★1/2	1929 Model A Roadster Pickup Truck
★★★	1929 Model A Closed Cab Pickup Truck
★★★	1929 Model A Panel Delivery
★★	1929 Model AA Truck

Momentum kept the new Model A going all through the 1928 model year and into the 1929 model year. There was still a very healthy demand for these cars, and Henry Ford could sell every one he could build. Even though he had everything going for him, in 1929 Henry Ford didn't want to leave anything to chance in this very competitive end of the market. Chevrolet would introduce its new six-cylinder engine

This 1929 Model A Roadster Pickup is equipped with a side-mounted spare tire, wind wings, and whitewall tires. *Elliott Kahn photo*

This 1929 Model A Fordor Sedan is done up in a nice two-tone color scheme with the darker color on top.

Like the Model Ts before it, the Model A chassis turned out to be a popular choice with fire equipment manufacturers. They liked the Model A's lightness, low price, and versatility.

Another Model A Roadster Pickup. This one is painted red with black fenders, wheels, and fabric top. *Elliott Kahn photo*

this year, and Plymouth sales were still doing well.

Henry Ford's plan for keeping his Model A a hot seller was to introduce some new models, one of which, the Model A Taxicab, was actually introduced late in the 1928 model year. This four-passenger, four-door sedan had a partition between the driver and passengers. Up front was one bucket seat, the taxi meter, and room to carry some luggage. In 1929, 4,857 Taxicabs were produced, each retailing at $800 (F.O.B. Detroit).

Another new Model A model in 1929 was the Cabriolet, a convertible with roll-up glass windows in its doors and a canvas top that could be raised or lowered in a matter of minutes. Both Briggs and Murray supplied the body. Also standard was a rumble seat to carry extra passengers. At a base price of $670 (F.O.B. Detroit), this proved to be a popular model, with 15,548 Cabriolets leaving the assembly lines.

In April 1929, Ford introduced still yet another new model to its Model A lineup. This vehicle was the first mass-produced, regular production line, station wagon offered by any manufacturer, the Model A Station Wagon. Before now, if a buyer wanted a station wagon, he bought a frame from one of the manufacturers and had an aftermarket "Depot Hack" body installed on the frame (sort of like an early model kit car). Murray used wood products from Ford's Iron Mountain plant to produce the completed bodies. The 1929 Model A Station Wagon was available at a base price of $695 (F.O.B. Detroit) and featured the same color of paint, Manila Brown, on both the hood and cowl.

You would think that Henry Ford had enough new models with the ones already mentioned to maintain a brisk sales pace, but he still had more to offer. One of these new models was the DeLuxe Delivery Car for businessmen who wanted an attractive closed car delivery vehicle. These cars would be called

A family goes out for a ride in their new 1929 Briggs-bodied Model A Fordor Sedan. This is one sharp-looking automobile, and no wonder—they were some of the most popular models Ford ever produced. *Ford Motor Company*

The Model A Fordor Sedan, like the one shown here, was always a top seller for Ford.

Another 1929 Model A Fordor Sedan. Note that this version uses a rubberized fabric top.

This particular 1928-29 Model A Closed Cab Pickup was seen in the 1994 edition of the Denver St. Patrick's Day Parade. Model A Fords, cars and trucks alike, are popular attractions in such events.

Sedan Deliveries because they looked so much like a regular passenger car sedan. The DeLuxe Delivery Car used a Tudor Sedan body, replacing the glass windows in the rear side windows area with steel panels; these panels would later be called "sign panels." Another unique feature was a large rear side-opening door cut into the back side of the body. Since this door precluded the use of a rear mounting, the spare tire was now carried in the left front fender.

1929 Prices (All prices listed are F.O.B. Detroit.)
Chassis: $350
Station Wagon: $695
Cabriolet: $670
Tudor Sedan: $535
Town Sedan: $695
Fordor Sedan: $625
Taxicab: $800
Town Car: $1,400
Roadster: $450
Phaeton: $460
Sport Coupe: $550
Coupe: $550

Bright yellow graces the exterior of this 1929 Model A Closed Cab Pickup. Besides the shocking paint it features a chromed grille, custom louvered hood, custom wheels, and tires.

Roadster Pickup Truck : $445
Closed Cab Pickup Truck : $495

These new models joined the Coupe, Business Coupe, Sport Coupe, Phaeton, Tudor, Town Car, and Fordor Sedans introduced the year before.

Fordor Sedan models this year were available with either two or three windows per side. The two-window versions had windows in the doors and a wide, covered rear "C" panel. These models were nicknamed the "Blind Back Sedans" because of the built-in blind spots on their roofs. This area on these

This 1929 Model A Coupe features a side-mounted spare tire, whitewall tires, and a rumble seat.

A rare Model A Town Car arrives at a Ford car show in California in 1994. It's a shame that more of these distinctive Model As aren't seen in car shows today.

Model A Coupes like this nifty-looking number are pretty popular in the collector car hobby these days. This one features fog lamps, radiator stone guard, and whitewall tires.

sedans was covered in a fabric or rubberized material. The three-window models had quarter windows located in this same area.

Back for a return engagement this year, the Model A Town Car was once again Ford's attempt to produce a car for customers who wanted a taste of luxury. Only 1,000 customers were willing to pay $1,400 for a ritzy version of Henry's Lady, and. this would be the last year that this body style would be carried in the Model A catalog. (That's why there aren't many of these cars still around for the Model A enthusiast who wants something a cut above the rest.)

Ford continued its plans for plant expansions in 1929, opening facilities in Turkey, Japan, South Africa, Australia, Germany, Holland, and Mexico. Furthermore, all Fordson Tractor production was moved to a Ford plant in County Cork, Irelandin 1929. During a ceremony held in Dagenham, England, in May of this year, Edsel Ford turned over the first shovelful of dirt at a site that would later become Ford's largest European assembly plant. The Fordson/Rouge assembly plant was renamed the Rouge Complex, and more passenger car and truck production was moved there.

In other related news, Henry Ford decided in 1929 to get out of the railroad business by his selling his interests in the Detroit, Toledo, and Ironton Railroad to a railroad company in Pennsylvania.

The Ford Motor Company celebrated the production of two milestone cars this year when the "Millionth" Model A came off the assembly lines in February 1929. That special event was followed by another, even more special, in July 1929, when the "Two Millionth" Model A was built.

Henry Ford celebrated another event in 1929 that had little to do with Ford automo-

A Model A Roadster Pickup. With the top down it's a sleek-looking street rod.

In 1929, this was called a Model A DeLuxe Delivery Car, but today it's referred to as a Sedan Delivery. Regardless of its real name, it is a sharp-looking automobile.

Model AA Ford truck fans can really appreciate a vintage photo like this which shows a loaded-down Model AA Coca Cola Truck. This truck would be a hit at car shows today.

If you think this Model A is an original from the 1920s, think again: it's a replica built in the mid-1970s. This car uses the drivetrain and other components from a Ford Pinto.

biles. This special event was in the form of a tribute to his good friend Thomas Alva Edison on the "Fiftieth Anniversary" of Edison's invention of the incandescent lightbulb. Henry Ford and hundreds of other celebrities gathered in Dearborn, Michigan, to open the Henry Ford Museum and Edison Institute. This unique complex housing a museum full of Americana and artifacts was Ford's gift to Americans to help them learn about and appreciate America's history. It was, and still is, the best display of Americana to be found anywhere.

Henry Ford, the Ford Motor Company, and Ford dealers had a lot to be happy about in 1929. Ford sold more cars and trucks this year than anybody else and it lookedas though they were back on top. It truly seemed that happy days had returned and that Ford would once again become the leader in the automotive world. Unfortunately, this euphoric feeling would last only a short time before the Great Depression would put a damper on everything.

A Model A owner who wanted his car to look sportier in the late 1920s might have opted to change its body for the "Collegian" version depicted in this ad. *Jerry Bougher Ads*

The New Ford Town Car

The new Ford Town Car is formal in appearance, with extremely precise lines. It is a personal car of intimate size, delightful convenience and unquestioned taste.

The body is custom-designed and finished in a choice of colors—new, in the modern mode, yet quietly restrained in tone. The back is square-cornered, in the Continental manner, with French landau leather rear quarters and rear panel.

Interior trimming is of English Bedford cords or French broadcloths—optional with the purchaser. The seat in the rear compartment is upholstered in the fashionable plain panel style, deeply cushioned and comfortable. Hardware is of distinctive scroll design, enameled to match the lining cloth. Accoutrements of the rear compartment include a vanity case mirror and notebook, clock, electric cigarette lighter and ash tray, center bow light and silk robe rail. Arm rests and individual hassocks are other pleasing features.

The chauffeur's compartment is upholstered in black leather and is separated from the passenger compartment by a glass partition, with sliding center window.

Triplex shatter-proof glass is used throughout the new Ford Town Car—for the windows and front glass partition, as well as the windshield. The transverse springs and four Houdaille hydraulic double-acting shock absorbers give unusual riding comfort. The price is $1400, f.o.b. Detroit, Michigan.

Ford Motor Company
Detroit, Michigan

For those who wanted a ritzy Model A there was the new Ford Town Car in 1929. This ad shows a rare car in a beautiful setting. *Jerry Bougher Ads*

Chapter 10

Refining Henry's Lady

1930	
★★★1/2	1930 Model A Victoria
★★★★1/2	1930 Model A DeLuxe Roadster
★★★★	1930 Model A Standard Roadster
★★★★1/2	1930 Model A Standard Phaeton
★★★★★	1930 Model A DeLuxe Phaeton
★★★★	1930 Model A Cabriolet
★★★1/2	1930 Model A Coupe
★★★1/2	1930 Model A DeLuxe Coupe
★★★1/2	1930 Model A Sport Coupe
★★★	1930 Model A Standard Tudor
★★★1/2	1930 Model A DeLuxe Tudor
★★★	1930 Model A Standard Fordor
★★★1/2	1930 Model A DeLuxe Fordor
★★★1/2	1930 Model A Town Sedan
★★★★	1930 Model A Station Wagon
★★★★1/2	1930 Model A Town Car Delivery
★★★★	1930 Model A DeLuxe Delivery
★★★1/2	1930 Model A Roadster Pickup Truck
★★★	1930 Model A Closed Cab Pickup Truck
★★★	1930 Model A Panel Delivery
★★	1930 Model AA Truck

The stock market crash of October 28–29, 1929, had a sobering effect on the American people and their buying habits. Gone were the days of free spending and devil-may-care attitudes. People were now worried about what the future might hold and became more conservative in their approach to making purchases. It was time to take a step back, take a deep breath, assess your options, and plan your future moves accordingly.

The new 1930 Fords made their debut on December 28, 1929, and for the first time since they were introduced two years before, these cars featured a new look. The previous 1928-1929 models used an exposed lower "A" pillar at the cowl which went from the base of the windshield down to the lower body edge. For 1930, Ford came up with a clever idea to hide this pillar—without compromising its importance to the overall structure of the body—by widening the cowl panel opening and having the cowl wrap around the pillars. The result was a much smoother and cleaner appearance. Ford also redesigned the belt moldings and changed the fender design a little bit. The radiator grille shell now was made of stainless steel rather than being a nickel-plated piece, and an extra piece of steel was painted body color and placed at the bottom of the shell. Also, since the radiator, hood, and cowl had been changed, the radiator grille shell was made a little taller so that its topmost edge was in a straight line to the cowl.

These changes were seen on the new 1930 Model A passenger cars. Commercial Cars such as the Station Wagon and Pickup Truck used carryover 1928-1929 front end pieces until that stock was used up and then switched over to the new 1930 styling.

For 1930, Ford decided to offer its customers the choice of a Standard line of cars as base models or, for a higher cost, a classier DeLuxe line. DeLuxe models were equipped with cowl lights, side-mounted spare tires, and other upgrades in trim or materials.

Standard versus DeLuxe Comparisons

Standard Roadster

Leatherette Interior Coverings
Black Fabric Top
Painted Windshield Frame
Trunk
Rear-Mounted Spare Tire

Cost: $435

DeLuxe Roadster

Real Leather Interior Coverings
Tan Fabric Top
Bright Metal Plated Windshield Frame
Rumble Seat in Place of Trunk
Side-Mounted Spare Tire in Fender Well
Windshield Wind Wings
Sideview Exterior Mirror
Luggage Rack
Cowl Lights
Cost: $520

This comparison shows standard equipment on both models; some of the DeLuxe equipment was available at extra cost for the Standard model. The difference in the base prices between the two versions, depending on model, ranged between $85 and $185. Ford started differentiating between the two versions as the Standard (Coupe, etc.) and the DeLuxe (Coupe, etc.) models in 1930a.

This 1930 Convertible Cabriolet is decked out with a radiator screen, whitewall tires, an accessory trunk, wind wings, and a Moto-Meter radiator cap.

A 1930 Model A Closed Cab Pickup (with later wheels) sits in a Colorado yard awaiting the day when someone finds it and begins a restoration.

The wheel size was reduced from 21in to 19in, which lowered the 1930 models at least an inch. Park an earlier model beside a 1930 version and you will notice that the newer car is smaller and because it sits lower sportier-looking.

In a move to liven up its lineup, Ford introduced three new models this year. The first new model was the DeLuxe Phaeton, a sportier rendition of the Standard Phaeton. There were several differences between the two. The Standard Phaeton was a four-door Touring Car that could seat up to six on two bench seats, whereas. the DeLuxe Phaeton was a two-door model with seating room for five (one less than the Standard because its front seats were two buckets rather than a wide single bench seat). The DeLuxe Phaeton also came equipped with cowl lights, a side-mounted spare tire, and a rear luggage rack, while the Standard model came with a rear-mounted spare tire, no luggage rack, and no cowl lights. The DeLuxe model retailed for $625, and the Standard Phaeton came in at $440.

The second new model was the Victoria, a close-coupled, two-door sedan with a shortened, stubby-looking body. It featured a canvas-covered top and looked quite a bit different than the regular Tudor Sedan. From some angles, the Victoria looked much sportier than the Tudor models. The Victoria was priced at $580 and was available only as a DeLuxe model.

The third new model, which was supposedly introduced late in the model year, was the Town Car Delivery. It was a fancier commercial delivery vehicle for businesses, and one that would appeal to the ritzy set. It was like a Model A Town Car for the commercial set. It was very similar in concept and execution to its fancy passenger car stablemate. It

Gab Joiner has run this 1930 Model A Roadster Pickup in a few Great American Races. Gab has added a number of accessories to his Model A to make it more comfortable, including a couple of seat cushions on the front bumper for people who might want to sit down and visit for a spell.

A couple of 1930 Model A Panel Deliveries on display at an American Truck Historical Society Show in California in 1990.

Red painted wheels add a sporty flair to a yellow 1930 Model A Convertible Cabriolet. Note that this car is equipped with a "Flying Quail" radiator cap, and a stone guard in front of the radiator.

Elliott Kahn found this 1930 Model A Fordor Sedan at a store in Florida in 1992. Its maroon painted body is highlighted with straw colored wheels. *Elliott Kahn photo*

had an open driver's compartment with a pull-out canvas top to protect the driver from the elements. The front seats were covered in the best leather, and on the inside of the cargo compartment, wood paneling and carpet protected the items being delivered. From the doors forward, the Town Car Delivery used regular Model A trim, including the doors, which were cut-down Tudor Sedan doors. From the doors back, it had a custom-crafted aluminum body built by Briggs to Ford specifications. The Town Car Delivery also featured a side-mounted spare tire, cowl lights, carriage lights mounted high on the side of the body, and other deluxe pieces. Because the Town Car Delivery cost around $1,150, only a few were produced in the 1930 model year.

In 1930, Ford opened new plants in Long Beach, California; Seattle, Washington; Buffalo, New York; and Edgewater, New Jersey. All automobile manufacturers saw their sales and production figures drop in 1930 due to the economic slump affecting the market, but the Model A again topped the sales charts and Ford stayed in the number one position. This was the second consecutive year that Ford was the best-selling car in the United States and the world.

This 1930 Model AA flatbed truck features a plated radiator shell usually found on passenger cars back in the Model A era. The normal grille shell for such a truck should be painted black.

Here is a beautiful 1930 Model A Type 150A Station Wagon. *Elliott Kahn photo*

You want to add a little brightness to the look of a 1930 Model A Fordor Sedan? Just add a set of vintage whitewall tires.

Model A Fords with Huckster bodies are a rare sight today. This one features a plated car radiator shell, side mounted spare tire, cowl lamps, and other goodies. *Elliott Kahn photo*

This 1930 Model A Station Wagon with side curtains in place ran in the Great American Race along with other Model A racers shown elsewhere in this book. Evidently the Great American Race is a popular racing venue for Model A owners.

A group of Model As gather together for a car show in California in the Spring of 1994.

This black 1930 Model A Closed Cab Pickup is dressed up with red painted wheels. *Elliott Kahn photo*

Model A Coupes like this one must be popular with restorers—you see so many of them on display at car shows throughout the country.

This Roadster model is typical of the great-looking pickup trucks Ford built in 1930. Note the black radiator shell, fenders, wheels, and windshield frame. *Elliott Kahn Photo*

When is the last time you saw a Model AA dump truck? This one showed up at an American Truck Historical Society Meet recently.

This 1930 Model A Closed Cab Pickup hot rod sits quite a bit lower than Henry and Edsel Ford envisioned it many years ago.

Here is another 1930 Model A Station Wagon. This time it's shown without the side curtains in place.

A group of Model A line up with a 1935 Ford at an antique car show in New Mexico in 1980.

This is one Model A fire engine that is truly decked out with all the "bells and whistles." Check out all those red lights and bells, and all the copper, chrome, and brass plating.

Elliott Kahn found this 1930 Model AA Ford Closed Cab flatbed truck in Clearwater, Florida in 1991. By the looks of it, this truck is in very good original condition and hasn't needed restoration yet. *Elliott Kahn photo*

Here is a 1930 Model A Ford Panel Delivery on display at an antique truck show in the late 1980s. Note fender-mounted spare tire and lightly colored wheels.

This 1930 Model A Ford Closed Cab Pickup wears a passenger car radiator shell in place of a black painted shell normally found on commercial vehicles of the period.

Model A Ford Roadster Pickups like this one from 1930 are popular with collectors. This one is equipped with options like a "Flying Quail" radiator cap, headlight deflectors, and a set of whitewall tires.

How would you like to have to drive around with a big sign like this on your car everyday. This Coca Cola route salesman probably didn't have a choice in the matter.

In 1930, this ad as used to introduce the new Tudor Sedan. The artwork used in these illustrations is nothing short of fantastic. *Carl King Ads*

Chapter 11

Henry's Lady Reaches the End of the Road

When the Model A was introduced to the public in December 1927, Edsel Ford predicted that it would be more popular than the Model T and would eclipse the Model T's mark of 15,000,000 units. It took the Model T more than nineteen years to reach that milestone mark, though, and there was no way Ford could afford to keep the Model A in production that long. Automobile shoppers had become more sophisticated and demanded new features, styling, and equipment changes, in addition to more models from which to choose. Chevrolet and Plymouth kept competition alive. Whether Edsel Ford liked it or not, the Model A would go down in the automotive history journals as an interim car that would bridge the gap between the Model T and the 1932 Ford V-8, the car that would make Ford the performance car champion of the low-priced three. The Model A remained in the lineup for only four years, and production numbers reached only one-third of what they were for

1931	
★★★★	1931 Model A Victoria
★★★★1/2	1931 Model A Standard Roadster

★★★★	1931 Model A DeLuxe Roadster
★★★★	1931 Model A Standard Phaeton
★★★★1/2	1931 Model A DeLuxe Phaeton
★★★★	1931 Model A Cabriolet
★★★★	1931 Model A Convertible Sedan
★★★	1931 Model A Standard Coupe
★★★1/2	1931 Model A DeLuxe Coupe
★★★1/2	1931 Model A Sport Coupe
★★★	1931 Model A Tudor Sedan
★★★1/2	1931 Model A DeLuxe Tudor Sedan
★★★	1931 Model A Standard Fordor
★★★1/2	1931 Model A DeLuxe Fordor
★★★1/2	1931 Model A Town Sedan
★★★★★	1931 Model A Town Car Delivery
★★★★	1931 Model A DeLuxe Delivery
★★★★	1931 Model A Roadster Pickup Truck
★★★1/2	1931 Model A Closed Cab Pickup Truck
★★★	1931 Model A Drop Floor Panel
★★★	1931 Model A Panel
★★★1/2	1931 Model A DeLuxe Panel
★★★★	1931 Model A DeLuxe Pickup Truck
★★★★	1931 Model A Station Wagon
★★★★	1931 Model A Natural Wood Delivery
★★	1931 Model AA Truck

This 1931 Model A Chassis/Windshield model features a special customer-installed body. United Parcel Service used this commercial car around the Long Beach, California area in 1931.

the Model T. For the Model A to have eclipsed the Model T record, Ford would have to sell 4,000,000 Model As each year for all the years it was produced. This wasn't going to happen in the late 1920s and early 1930s. As it was, Ford sold and produced five million Model As during its four-year history.

The Model A wasn't going to go quietly into the night, however. Just the opposite was true. Instead of retreating to a safe, passive position, the 1931 line of Fords was marketed aggressively from the moment they were released in late fall 1930 until the last US-built models were produced in early 1932.

Once again, Ford offered some new models to draw people back into its showrooms. Its newest model, a chic 1931 Model A Convertible Sedan, was a beautiful sporty-looking automobile. The beauty of this car was that its passengers were protected from the elements with glass windows in the doors, and they could have lots of sunshine and fresh air by lowering the canvas top. Ford designated this car as its Type 400-A Convertible Sedan. All of these cars were DeLuxe models, so they came with side-mounted spare tires and cowl lights, and since they were introduced in May 1931, they all featured Ford's new slanting windshield post design. An estimated 5,000 units were produced.

The Town Car Delivery returned again this year as a special model, but even with a few more new customers, it didn't make much of an impression on the sales or production charts. In 1931, only 190 of them were produced, and only a half dozen or so were recorded in 1930—which means that fewer than 200 units were built for both model years. That might explain why so few are seen today. The cost of $1,150 (F.O.B. Detroit) might have had something to do with those low sales numbers, as it was more than twice what a Model A DeLuxe Delivery went for. The DeLuxe Delivery was a fine-looking vehicle reasonably priced at $540, which is why 9,500 or so were produced in 1931.

The Model A Station Wagon with its natural wood body was still available in 1931 as one of Ford's Commercial Car. This "woodie" wasn't that popular a vehicle in Ford's lineup, due to its cost and also because of all the work that was needed to keep its natural wood body in tip-top shape, but Ford decided to introduce a new Station Wagon variant this year. Ford called this new vehicle the Natural Wood Panel Delivery, or the Type 255-A Special Delivery. Its natural wood body looked like the Station Wagon and was provided by the Baker-Raulang Company, a contract body supplier to

Model A "Huckster" Pickups, like this 1931 model, were rare in their day, and are even more rare today.

This shot of a 1931 Model A Victoria Soft Roof model shows the padding on the roof and rear-mounted luggage carrier.

One of the best-looking Model As produced during the era was the 1931 Convertible Sedan like the one shown here. Its owner has even gone so far as to display its tool kit in front of the car. *Elliott Kahn photo*

Ford. However, it was a two-door model, whereas the Station Wagon came with four doors. It also had roll-up glass windows in the doors, while the Station Wagon still used side curtains instead of windows. The Special Delivery also didn't have any side windows–that area was covered instead by wooden sign panels. The original cost of a Natural Wood Panel Delivery was a little more than $600. Don't you wish you could buy one for that price today?

The Natural Wood Panel Delivery wasn't the only new special commercial vehicle Ford offered this year. Another new, unique commercial vehicle introduced in 1931 was the Model A DeLuxe Pickup Truck, featuring a unique custom-crafted bed that was wrapped around the rear portion of the cab, making the two units look like they were one piece. The bed was actually bolted to the back of the cab with hidden carriage bolts. Other unique features found on this bed included its wooden lining, chrome-plated brass rails, and a special tailgate. Also, the regular Model A Pickup Truck featured a restyled bed this year. This was the first time this bed had been redone since the mid-1920s.

The Model A DeLuxe Pickup Truck wasn't the only new pickup Ford offered this year. Another new model seen in Ford's Commercial Car line in 1931 was the Canopy Top Pickup Truck, which used a regular pickup box to which was added a frame, roof panel, and side curtains. This was a popular choice for the street merchants of the day who sold their wares from the backs of trucks.

Ford still offered a regular Panel Delivery in 1931 and decided to expand this model by introducing a new version called the Drop Floor Panel, which had a lowered floor back behind the rear wheels. Dropping the floor in this area gave an increase in the height of the cargo box for businesses that needed a few extra inches for their cargo, such as dry cleaners and laundries. Although the idea certainly had merit, this was the only year that this model would be available. Evidently, Ford didn't sell enough of them to keep them in the catalogs.

1931 Prices (All prices listed are F.O.B. Detroit.)
Station Wagon: $650
Town Sedan: $670
Cabriolet: $645
DeLuxe Tudor: $525
DeLuxe Fordor Sedan: $600
Victoria: $725
Convertible Sedan: $640
Town Car DeLuxe: $1,150
Standard Phaeton: $435
Standard Roadster: $430
DeLuxe Roadster: $475

Dale Lewis, of Albuquerque, New Mexico, owns this restored 1931 Model A Closed Cab Pickup. This truck's headlights have been replaced by sealed beam units, and its horn has been chrome plated: slight modifications to make the truck a little more appealing.

Here is an example of a Model AA flatbed truck. Note black painted radiator shell which was used on commercial vehicles during the Model A era.

A group of Model As line up at a car show. Shown are a Model A Standard Coupe, Model A Roadster, and a Tudor Sedan. Note "Flying Quail" radiator cap.

Note that this 1931 Model A Closed Cab Pickup wears a plated, car-type, grille shell. This truck also uses sealed beam headlamps that weren't available in 1931. *Elliott Kahn photo*

This 1931 Model A Coupe features a mesh grille guard, rumble seat, whitewall tires, and a "Flying Quail" radiator cap.

Standard Tudor: $490
Standard Coupe: $490
DeLuxe Coupe: $525
Sport Coupe: $500
DeLuxe Phaeton: $580

Ford also offered two Victoria models this year: a canvas-topped model as they did in 1930, or a steel-topped version that was new for this year. Some people think that the latter version looks much nicer than the former.

There were two versions of the 1931 Model A. The first version debuted in January 1931 and looked pretty much the same as the 1930 models it replaced. The second version, referred to now as the 1931-1/2 model, looked a little different, especially in the windshield area. The earlier version used vertical windshield posts, while the latter used slanted ones. Ford consequently did away with the sunvisors that were part and parcel of its closed models since day one. Ford introduced this change to the Model A line in April 1931.

Another new feature found on the 1931 Model A passenger cars was the body color-painted insert at the top of the radiator shell. This painted panel makes it pretty easy to tell these models apart from their earlier offerings. Like the 1930 models, they also used a painted insert at the bottom of the radiator shell. This panel could have been painted body color or black.

Ford opened plants in Dagenham, England; and Cologne, Germany as well as a new plant in Richmond, California, which produced cars for Northern and Central California, Hawaii, Tahiti, Guam, and American Samoa.

The Ford Motor Company of Canada celebrated a milestone event with the production

Another 1931 Model A DeLuxe Coupe in a two-tone finish. Note the whitewall tires, Moto-Meter radiator cap, rumble seat, and a step plate on the running-board.

Here is a Model AA Stake Bed Truck. To add a little glitter to the front end of his truck, its owner has replaced the black painted radiator shell with a plated car type.

This patriotic, flag-draped, 1931 Model A Victoria Coupe features a steel roof. In addition to this steel roof version, a soft padded top version was also available this year.

of its "Millionth" Ford. In the United States, the Ford Motor Company celebrated when its "20,000,000th" Ford, a Fordor Sedan, rolled off the line at Dearborn, Michigan, on April 14, 1931. This car then went on a national promotional tour across the country, visiting hundreds of cities and towns.

Henry Ford stopped production of the Model A in July 1931, but there were enough cars in the pipeline to be sure that Ford dealers had enough cars to keep them going until the new Ford V-8 would debut in March 1932.

Records show that calendar year production of the 1931 Model A numbered a little more than 541,600 units before the plants were shut down in late July 1931. Records also show that during that same time, about 528,580 Model As were sold. That means that 13,000 cars were sold after 1931, with most of those sales coming in that interim period before the "Deuce" arrived.

Some people think that this, the final year of Model A production, was the Model A's finest hour. They point to the fact that Ford offered more models and more value to the buyer this year. Whether you agree with this notion really doesn't matter. What matters is that the Model A was one of the best Fords ever built, and that might explain why there has always been a warm spot in our hearts for "Henry's Lady."

This is a "Steel Top" Victoria Coupe. Compare this top to the soft top version.

Two Model A Pickups shown side by side. The customized version is a 1928-29 model, while the stock version is a 1931 Model A Closed Cab pickup.

This 1931 Model A Closed Cab Pickup is shod with later model Early Ford V8 wheels. Compare the wheels and tires on the ground with the stock type mounted in the fender well.

Rom Barnes started his 1931 Ford Model A hot rod project as a sophomore in high school back in 1958. The hot rod, which was finally completed in 1991, is a popular attraction wherever it appears.

Sedan Delivery models don't get much better-looking than this 1931 Model A DeLuxe Delivery Car. *Ford Motor Company*

There isn't much room in a Model A Roadster for a family to travel in even with the luxury of having a rumble seat. A separate trunk can come in pretty handy to carry one's belongings in such a situation

A recently restored 1931 Ford Model A Victoria Coupe sits on display at the San Diego Automotive Museum in that city's historic Balboa Park. This museum has many beautiful and interesting cars.

Whitewall tires weren't seen on many Model A Pickups in 1931. However, the addition of whitewalls on this dark green truck really brightens it up.

One of the sharpest-looking Model A Fords of the era has to be the 1931 Model A Convertible Sedan.

Here is a family out for an afternoon drive in their new 1931 Model A Fordor Sedan.

As far as commercial vehicles go they don't come any classier than this 1931 Model A DeLuxe Delivery car.

Epilogue

Unlike that for other cars, interest in Model Ts and Model As didn't die off when the Ford Motor Company ceased producing them. For a few years thereafter, they were part and parcel of the usual used car market. They were popular cars, providing cheap, affordable, dependable transportation for people who couldn't or wouldn't buy new cars.

People fixed them up with parts and pieces from Ford dealers, aftermarket parts stores, and a growing number of junkyards. Some of these same people were tinkerers looking to improve the looks or the performance of their cars. Some of them just swapped parts with parts from other cars to make their cars look a little different. Some Model T owners used Model A parts to help upgrade their cars, and some Model A owners, in turn, used replacement parts from early Ford V8 cars. Some of those changes even included removing the old venerable Ford four-cylinder engine and dropping in a Ford V8. Thus were sown the seeds for what would become the hot rod movement later on.

During the late 1940s two new movements in the world of automobiles gained momentum in the United States. Both movements would be started by individuals who were interested in Model Ts or Model As. One group's primary interest was in modifying cars to make them more modern, while the other group's intentions were to restore the cars 100 per cent back to original condition.

As you can well imagine, since these goals were 180 degrees apart, conflicts soon arose between the groups. With both groups going after a dwindling supply of cars, there wasn't much room for compromise. Both movements grew and prospered during the 1950s, attracting new converts to their respective folds with each passing year.

The hot rod movement reached its peak in the early 1960s primarily because Detroit started offering its own factory-built Hot Rods in the form of muscle cars and there wasn't any reason to go to the trouble of building your own piece of "Vintage Tin" from a rusted-out hulk. With interest in hot rods declining, restorers found more cars to work on, and their numbers grew with every car show. The number of restored Model Ts and Model As also started to grow, and it was a rare show that didn't feature at least a handful of these cars. The restoration movement hit its stride in the early 1970s, and before too long, the Model As became the number one favorite among collectors.

A nostalgia craze came on strong in the late 1970s and with it a renewed interest in all cars. Once again, the Model As were at the forefront of this new craze. Heading up the renewed interest in hot rods were the same people who built them some twenty years before: matured hot rodders who were trying to recreate the good times they had when they were younger. The driving force in the restoration ranks was now being supplied by an influx of new, younger enthusiasts who wanted to recreate their own little piece of Americana. Both groups are still growing by leaps and bounds, and in most cases have learned to accept one another's views and to appreciate their common love for old cars. Some of these people have both a restored car and a hot rod, and will even show them together.

Henry Ford and son Edsel would be happy to know that the love of automobiles they sparked is still growing strong. When the first of fifteen million Model T Fords rolled off the assembly lines some eighty-five years ago, Henry Ford did more than build the first car for the common man. He changed the mindset of a nation. And with the release of the first of four and one-half million Model As in December 1927, he and Edsel guaranteed that these cars would remain two of the most influential cars that ever turned a wheel on the highways and byways of the world.

Appendices

Recycled Plants

One of my favorite pastimes as a young man growing up in Cambridge, Massachusetts, during the 1950s was visiting the Ford assembly plant in neighboring Somerville. This sprawling complex drew me much as a moth is drawn to a flame or a light bulb. I couldn't resist the lure because even at such a young age, I was already a staunch Ford enthusiast.

While my peers enjoyed playing sports or watching television, I reveled in wandering around this huge complex, looking at all the then-new Fords and lineups of Ford car carriers that would deliver them to dealers all over the New England area. Had the plant stayed open, I probably would have ended up driving one of those rigs one day, helping deliver Fords near and far. Unfortunately, though, in 1958, Ford decided to close this facility and move its operations to New Jersey. It was a black day for the plant, the people who worked there, the city of Somerville, and me.

After Ford left, the property and buildings were bought by the First National Food Stores chain, which used the facility as a distribution point for all its New England stores. When First National was done with it in the 1970s, the property was used as a storage facility for some of the car dealers in the immediate area. After they were done with it, the property sat idle until it was bought by some real estate developers, who turned it into a shopping mall. Today, the property is known as Assembly Line Mall and one can still see evidence of the plant's origins while strolling through the complex.

Unbeknownst to me in the 1950s, another Ford plant in the Boston area preceded the Somerville facility. This plant, located along Memorial Drive in Cambridge, was in operation during the Model T era. I had passed this plant at least 100 times before learning that it, too, started life as a Ford assembly plant. I learned about this from stories told to me by an old Ford salesman in the 1960s.

The Memorial Drive plant was built in 1913 along the banks of the Charles River opposite the Boston University Bridge, which afforded the plant easy access to Boston's "Automobile Row" along Commonwealth Avenue on the west side of the river. The five-story plant's major building was quite an eye-catching sight, especially in the late afternoon when the setting sun was reflected in its many windows. At sunset, the orange glow gave the plant an ethereal effect. This 200,000sq-ft facility assembled cars from parts shipped to it from Detroit. As part of the assembly process, the cars were road tested on a track laid out on the roof of the plant before they were released.

The plant stayed in operation from 1913 through 1927, when it was closed and production was moved to the Somerville facility where the Model A Ford bowed in late 1927. Ford kept the plant for a few years after that until it was sold to a new tenant in 1933. Then in the late 1940s, the Polaroid Corporation bought the complex, using it until moving to new quarters in the 1980s. Since then, the complex has languished in uncertainty until its present owner, the Massachusetts Institute of Technology (MIT), decided what to do with it. This once-proud plant was falling into decay at the hands of vandals and owner neglect—a sad sight to behold.

About five years ago, I visited this complex and took note of all the damage the buildings had suffered. I wished that someone, myself included, might have the wherewithal to rescue this historic facility from such an ignoble fate. I thought a building with as much history as this one should be saved and refurbished for future Ford enthusiasts to enjoy. My wish is coming true.

In 1992, MIT decided that the time had come to do something with the old Ford plant. Instead of knocking it down to make room for a parking lot or a new dormitory, they decided to gut the inside of the building and restore the exterior, with minimal changes, to what it looked like some eighty years ago. MIT has already committed $13,000,000 to turn this eyesore back into the proud building it was in its glory days.

The restoration project was scheduled to be completed in fall 1993, when the building would be turned over to a new tenant. Although it is rather doubtful that Ford cars will ever be built in this plant again, it is nice to know that this plant still has a future in Cambridge and that future Ford enthusiasts can enjoy it as much as an old Ford enthusiast has for many years.

Trinkets and Treasures

Due to the immense popularity of both the Model T and Model A, anything related to either car, from tools to photographs and everything in between, is collectible today. If you like paper goods, you might consider starting a collection of Model T and Model A sales literature. Depending on their rarity, original pieces in excellent condition can cost you dearly, but nice reproduction pieces are more reasonably priced. Not everything has been reproduced, though, so if you want a particular piece, you may have to pay the

Note the intricate carved wings on this "Moto-Meter" styled Model T radiator cap.

higher price. Other paper goods worthy of consideration are the many magazine ads that are available from a number of dealers. Most of the Model T ads are done in black-and-white, but during the Model A era, Ford advertised in several magazines, using colorfully painted illustrations that are works of art. These pieces look wonderful when framed and displayed. Many magazine ad dealers also offer sales literature, which may be ordered through the mail, or available at one of the hundreds of swap meets held around the country every year. Still other paper goods you might want to collect are the many shop manuals, owners manuals, and technical bulletins that were released during the Model T and Model A eras. These items perform two functions: they look great in a display around your car, and they can come in handy when you are working on a mechanical problem or doing some restoration work.

A close up look at a Frontenac Overhead Valve conversion on a Model T engine. This head, produced by the Chevrolet brothers, was one of the best designs of its type.

No Ford reference library would be complete without at least one Model T and Model A book on hand. Over the years, many good books on both series of cars have been published. Don't despair if you are looking for an out-of-print book, as even they aren't that hard to find.

If miniature cars appeal to you, you'll be happy to know that many Model T and Model A toys and models have been released over the years. Not long after Henry Ford released his Model T, several toy makers began releasing their own smaller versions. Some of them look pretty realistic—especially the cast-iron Arcade Model Ts, which are now the most famous, and Model As. These toys can bring pretty hefty prices at antique toy shows, but occasionally one pops up at an antique store or flea market. If you can't afford one of these gems, don't despair, because some toymakers are offering reasonably priced reproductions of these originals.

1990s version of a Model T Ford Roadster Pickup. Wide rear tires, light-weight, and a hot modern V-8 give this Model T a lot of potential for producing one wild ride.

If you don't need or want a sixty- or seventy-year-old toy in your collection, you might want to concentrate on Model T and Model A toys and models released in the last twenty or twenty-five years. There have been some great items released during this era and they are all more affordable than the earlier versions. If built-up, already-assembled models appeal to you, look for the models released by Ertl, Matchbox, Corgi, Hot Wheels, and the like. If you want to build your own model, look for those made by Revell, Monogram, AMT, Ertl, Aurora, Airfix, Entex, Lindburg, and others. You might be surprised by how many Model T and Model A miniatures that you can acquire with relative ease.

Automotive art is a new phenomenon to catch on in the old car collector hobby. Several artists and art dealers carry Model T- and Model A-themed pieces. Photographs of Model Ts and Model As can also be purchased, framed, and displayed.

Images of Model Ts and Model As have appeared on other collectibles, too, such as plates, trays, cups, jewelry, calendars, belt buckles, and t-shirts. You might also consider collecting stamps, matchbooks, postcards, games, and puzzles which use likenesses of these vehicles.

Tool collecting can also be great fun. During both the Model T and Model A era, Henry Ford released many tools, most of which have the Ford name or script stamped on them. A complete tool kit can really add to a Model T or a Model A display. And don't forget that a collection of period clothing or accessories is interesting too.

The best thing about most Model T and Model A collectibles is that they are affordable. All you have to do is to go to a swap meet or car show, order what you want from one of the dealers who specialize in these kinds of things, or just look in the classified sections of one of the hobby publications. You're sure to find just about anything you want. Happy collecting.

Frontenac Ford Highlights
- Louis Chevrolet in 1923 designed and produced his first Frontenac DO head for the Model T.
- Fronty-Fords, as they were called, ran at the Indianapolis 500, but never won this prestigious event. However, they were the scourge of the dirt tracks that dominated the American landscape in the 1920s, winning most of the time.
- The Chevrolet brothers produced about 10,000 Frontenac heads during the 1920s.
- In 1922, two Fronty-Fords were entered in the Indianapolis 500, where they finished in fourteenth and eighteenth place, respectively.
- In 1923, the Barber-Warnock Special Fronty-Ford entry finished a credible fifth in the race, running against mostly faster, more powerful, more exotic entries.
- The Model R hea was released in 1922. This version featured one inlet and three exhaust ports per cylinder and case-hardened rocker arms.
- The Model DO head had dual intake and exhaust ports, four valves per cylinder, two spark plugs per cylinder, and dual chain-driven camshafts.
- This Model T Fronty head version was made available for street-driven cars; all other versions were meant to be used on race cars only. The Fronty T head doubled the stock engine's horsepower rating of 20.
- The Model SR head used all the same pieces as the R, S, and DO heads, but provided two inlets for dual carb usage and two spark plugs per cylinder.
- The Model S head (S for Sportster) was similar to the R head
- The Model T (Street Version or Touring) head was available complete for $99 in the mid 1920s.

Model A Assembly Process
Bare frame
Brake parts added to frame
Running board brackets installed on frame
More brake parts installed on frame
Engine support brackets mounted on frame
Shock absorbers assembled mounted on frame
Two front fender brackets installed on frame
Front spring and assorted parts and spindles attached to front axle on separate line
Assembled front axle assembly installed on frame
Rear spring assembly bolted in place at rear of frame
Rear axle housing bolted to rear spring

A young Ed Roth, famed car customizer, with one of his early Model T Ford-based customs.

More brake parts added to frame
Frame assembly painted in black paint
Front brake shoes, backing plates, and drums assembled
Front wheel bearings installed and filled with grease
Brake pedal equalizer shaft attached to left-hand brake cross-shaft assembly
Rear axle housing filled with lubricant
Complete rear axle brake assemblies, right and left, attached to rear axle housing
Chassis inspected
Front brake assemblies added to front axle
Pre-assembled engine dropped into place on frame
Motor number stamped onto engine block
Engine pan bolted to oil pan boss and front cross-member

Touch-up paint applied on chassis where necessary
Front radius-rod ball attached to clutch housing
Axle shaft nuts tightened
Four pre-assembled wheel and tire combinations installed on car
Four bracket bolts and two front cross-member bolts installed on engine
Nuts on rear engine support tightened
All hoses and fittings attached to radiator assembly
Radiator assembly installed on frame with bolts and pads
Front bumper assembly bolted to front end of frame
All brake cables, clevices, cotter pins, nuts, bolts, springs, and the like installed on

Model T magazine advertisements like this one make a nice addition to any literature collection. *Jerry Bougher Ads*

frame
Hand brake lever assembly fitted to frame
Steering gear assembly, shaft, and attachments mounted on frame
Muffler assembly and exhaust system mounted on frame
Battery support assembly installed on frame
Rear bumper pieces attached to rear of frame
All fittings greased
Radiator assembly mounted on frame and radiator filled with water
Battery installed and cables hooked up and tightened
Right and left front fenders bolted to running board shields
Fenders and running boards painted
Fender and running aboard assemblies fitted to brackets on frame
Two headlights mounted on headlight bar, one horn mounted on front fender
Rear fenders, wheel carrier assembly, and taillight mounted on body
Pre-painted and trimmed body dropped on frame and running board assembly
Frame mounts and bolts installed and tightened
Radiator to firewall rods installed
Hood clip assemblies and attachments mounted to frame
Front splash shield assembly attached to front of frame
Hood assembly painted to match body color
Rod assemblies for carburetor, spark control, and the like, assembled between carburetor and distributor
Wiring connected to headlights, horn, starter, generator, and other electrical systems
Painted hood matched to body and installed
Miscellaneous trim items installed
Floor coverings installed
Fuel put in fuel tank
Engine started and car driven off assembly line
Final inspection

A Model T Speedster project awaits completion at the San Diego Auto Museum. These are fun projects that allow a lot of creativity.

Completed cars driven to storage lots awaiting delivery

Model T Options

Ford didn't offer much in the way of factory options to the Model T buyer from 1908 through 1927. That was left up to the aftermarket. The few items that Ford sold through his dealers and agents were:
Bumpers
Prestolite headlights (electric)
Headlights (some Model Ts didn't come with any)
Tire chains
Spare tire carrier
Horns
Speedometer
Electric starter (starting in 1919 on closed cars)
Demountable rims (starting in 1919 on closed cars)
Top boot cover
Windshield wipers (starting in 1926)
Wind wings (starting in 1925)
Wire wheels (starting in 1925)
Shock absorbers (starting in 1926)
Rear stop light (starting in 1926)

Model A Exterior Colors

Unlike the Model T, which came only in black, the Model A was available in a wide variety of exterior colors.

To better understand the choices and color combinations available, it is helpful to first understand some of the terms used to describe different areas of the body:

Reveals: Area surrounding the windows between the belt molding and top.

Belt molding: The molding below the windows that separates upper and lower body areas.

Upper body: The area above the belt molding, including the top.

Lower Body: The area below the belt molding, including the hood and cowl.

Stripe: Accent striping used to accentuate body lines or moldings.

All fenders and splash aprons on the Model A were painted black. Wheels were also painted black, unless otherwise noted.

1928 Model A Fordor and Town Sedan

Lower Body	Upper Body	Belt Molding	Stripe	Reveals
Balsam Green	Valley Green	Balsam Green	Old Ivory	
Copra Drab	Seal Brown	Copra Drab		Orange
Rose Beige	Seal Brown	Rose Beige		Orange
Andalusite Blue	Arabian Sand	Orange		

1928 Roadster and Phaeton

Lower Body	Upper Body	Belt Molding	Stripe	Reveals
Niagara Blue (Lt or Dk)	Duchess Blue	French Gray		
Arabian Sand (Lt or Dk)	Copra Drab	French Gray		
Dawn Gray	Gunmetal Blue	French Gray		
Gunmetal Blue	Chelsea Blue	Straw		

1928 Tudor Sedan, Coupe, Sport Coupe

Lower Body	Upper Body	Belt Molding	Stripe	Reveals
Niagara Blue (Lt)	Niagara Blue (Dk)	Duchess Blue	French Gray (Dk)	
Arabian Sand (Dk)	Copra Drab		French Gray	French Gray
Dawn Gray	Gunmetal Blue	Dawn Gray		Straw
Niagara Blue (Dk) (Lt)	Niagara Blue (Lt)	Duchess Blue		French Gray
Niagara Blue (Lt)	Duchess Blue			French Gray
Gunmetal Blue	Black		French Gray	French Gray

1928 Commercial Cars (Pickup Trucks, Panel Trucks, etc.)

Lower Body	Upper Body	Radiator Shell
Rock Moss Green	Black	French Gray

1929 Roadster and Phaeton

Lower Body	Upper Body	Belt Molding	Stripe	Reveals
Bonnie Gray	Chelsea Blue	Straw		
Rose Beige	Seal Brown	Orange		
Balsam Green	Valley Green	Medium Green		
Andalusite Blue	Black	French Gray		

1929 Coupe and Tudor Sedan

Lower Body	Upper Body	Belt Molding	Stripe	Reveals
Bonnie Gray	Bonnie Gray	Straw	Chelsea Blue	Straw
Vagabond Green	Vagabond Green	Straw	Rock Moss Green	Straw
Rose Beige	Rose Beige	Straw	Seal Brown	Straw
Andalusite Blue	Black	French Gray	Niagara Blue	French Gray

1929 Town Car

Lower Body	Upper Body	Belt Molding	Stripe	Reveals
Thorne Brown	Black	Black	Orange	Thorne Brown
Black	Black	Black	Gold	
Brewster Green	Black	Black	Apple Green	Brewster Green

1929 Taxicab

Lower Body	Upper Body	Belt Molding	Hood	Cowl	Reveals
Balsam Green	Black	Cream	Black	Balsam	Green
Duchess Blue	Black	Cream	Black	Duchess	Blue

1929 Commercial
Lower Body	Upper Body	Radiator Shell
Rock Moss Green	Black	French Gray

1929 Fordor Sedan and Town Sedan
Lower Body	Upper Body	Belt Molding	Stripe	Reveals
Bonnie Gray	Chelsea Blue	Chelsea Blue	Straw	Bonnie Gray
Vagabond Green	Rock Moss Green	Rock Moss Green	Straw	Vagabond Green
Andalusite Blue	Andalusite Blue	Andalusite Blue	French Gray	Niagara Blue
Rose Beige	Seal Brown	Seal Brown	Straw	Rose Beige

1929 Station Wagon
Hood Assembly	Cowl Assembly
Manila Brown	Manila Brown

1930 Station Wagon
Hood Assembly	Cowl Assembly
Manila Brown	Manila Brown

1930 Cabriolet
Lower Body	Upper Body	Belt Molding	Stripe	Reveals
Andalusite Blue	Andalusite Blue	French Gray		
Moleskin Brown	Moleskin Brown	Tacoma	Cream	
Elkpoint Green	Kewanee Green	Kewanee Green	Apple Green	Elkpoint Green

Lower Body	Upper Body	Belt Molding	Deck Lid	Reveals
Bronson Yellow	Seal Brown	Orange	Seal Brown	Bronson Yellow

1930 Phaeton and Roadster
Lower Body	Upper Body	Belt Molding	Stripe	Reveals
Thorne Brown	Thorne Brown	Straw		
Copra Drab	Chicle Drab	Straw		
Andalusite Blue	Andalusite Blue	French Gray		
Elkpoint Green	Kewanee Green	Apple Green		

1930 Sport Coupe, Standard Coupe, Tudor Sedan
Lower Body	Upper Body	Belt Molding	Stripe	Reveals
Thorne Brown	Thorne Brown	Orange		
Andalusite Blue	Black	Black	French Gray	Andalusite Blue
Copra Drab	Chicle Drab	Chicle Drab	Straw	Copra Drab
Elkpoint Green	Kewanee Green	Kewanee Green	Apple Green	Elkpoint Green

1930 Fordor Sedans
Lower Body	Upper Body	Belt Molding	Stripe	Reveals
Thorne Brown	Thorne Brown	Thorne Brown	Orange	
Copra Drab	Chicle Drab	Chicle Drab	Straw	Chicle Drab

1930 DeLuxe Sedan
Lower Body	Upper Body	Belt Molding	Stripe	Reveals
Elkpoint Green	Kewanee Green	Kewanee Green	Apple Green	Elkpoint Green
Ford Maroon	Black	Black	Vermillion Red	Maroon
Andalusite Blue	Black	Black	French Gray	Andalusite Blue

1930 Town Sedan

Lower Body	Upper Body	Belt Molding	Stripe	Reveals
Copra Drab	Chicle Drab	Chicle Drab	Straw	Copra Drab
Ford Maroon	Black	Black	Vermillion Red	Maroon

1930 Commercial

Lower Body	Upper Body	Radiator Shell
Rock Moss Green	Rock Moss Green	Black

1931 Station Wagon

Hood Assembly	Cowl Assembly
Manila Brown	Manila Brown

1931 Commercial

Lower Body	Upper Body	Radiator Shell
Rock Moss Green	Rock Moss Green	Black

1931 Coupe, Tudor, Fordor Sedans

Lower Body	Upper Body	Belt Molding	Stripe	Reveals
Black	Black	Black	Apple Green	
Kewanee Green	Elkpoint Green	Elkpoint Green	Apple Green	Elkpoint Green
Thorne Brown	Black	Black	French Gray	Black
Lombard Blue	Black	Black	French Gray	Black
Chicle Drab	Copra Drab	Copra Drab	Straw	Chicle Drab

1931 Convertible Sedan

Lower Body	Upper Body	Belt Molding	Reveals	Wheels
Copra Drab	Copra Drab	Straw	Chicle Drab	Straw

Lower Body	Upper Body	Belt Molding	Stripe	Wheels
Washington Blue	Riviera Blue		Tacoma Cream	Tacoma Cream
Brewster Green			Vermillion Red	Vermillion

1931 DeLuxe Roadster and DeLuxe Phaeton

Lower Body	Upper Body	Belt Molding	Stripe	Wheels
Washington Blue	Riviera Blue		Tacoma Cream	Tacoma Cream
Lombard Blue			Duchess Blue	Duchess Blue
Black			Apple Green	Apple Green

1931 DeLuxe Roadster

Lower Body	Upper Body	Belt Molding	Stripe	Wheels
Stone Brown	Stone Gray		Tacoma Cream	Tacoma Cream
Brewster Green	Black		Apple Green	Apple Green

1931 Standard Roadster and Phaeton

Lower Body	Upper Body	Belt Molding	Stripe	Reveals
Thorne Brown	Straw			
Chicle Drab	Straw			
Lombard Blue	Duchess Blue			
Kewanee Green	Elkpoint Green	Apple Green		
Black	Apple Green			

1931 DeLuxe Town Sedan, DeLuxe Coupe, Victoria

Lower Body	Upper Body	Belt Molding	Stripe	Reveals
Black	Black	Black	Apple Green	
Kewanee Green	Elkpoint Green	Elkpoint Green	Apple Green	Kewanee Green
Brewster Green	Black	Black	Apple Green	Brewster Green
Chicle Drab	Copra Drab	Straw	Straw	Straw
Ford Maroon	Black	Black	Vermillion Red	Maroon

1931 Cabriolet

Lower Body	Upper Body	Belt Molding	Stripe	Reveals	Wheels
Ford Maroon	Black		Vermillion Red	Black	Vermillion
Black			Apple Green		Apple Green
Brewster Green	Black	Black	Apple Green	Brewster Green	Apple Green
Kewanee Green		Elkpoint Green	Apple Green	Elkpoint Green	Apple Green
Bronson Yellow	Seal Brown	Seal Brown	Orange	Bronson Yellow	
Lombard Blue	Duchess Blue				
Moleskin Brown	Seal Brown	Seal Brown	French Gray	Seal Brown	

In the early days of the auto collecting hobby there weren't many books available on the subject. However, most of what was available was published by the late Floyd Clymer.

Magazine ads like this one for a Model T Sedan make nice collectibles. They can be kept in albums or matted and framed.

Model A Ford Models and Model Numbers

1928-1929

Model Number	Name	Description
35-A	Phaeton	
40-A	Roadster	
45-A	Coupe	
49-A	Special Coupe	
50-A	Sport Coupe	
54-A	Business Coupe	
55-A	Tudor Sedan	
60-A	Fordor Sedan	Leather Back Seal Brown Top (Briggs)
60-B	Fordor Sedan	Leather Back Black Top (Briggs)
60-C	Fordor Sedan	Steel Back Top 1929 (Briggs)
68-A	Cabriolet	1929
140-A	Town Car	
150-A	Station Wagon	1929
155-A	Town Sedan	1929 (Murray)
165-A	Fordor Sedan	1929 (Murray)
165-B	Fordor Sedan	1929 (Briggs)
170-A	Fordor Sedan	1929 two-window
170-B	Fordor Sedan	1929 two-window
79-A	Panel Delivery	103.5in wheelbase
78-A	Pickup Truck	
130-A	DeLuxe Delivery	1929
135-A	Taxicab	1929

1930

Model Number	Name	Description
35-B	Standard Phaeton	
40-B	Standard Roadster	
40-B	DeLuxe Roadster	
45-B	Standard Coupe	
45-B	DeLuxe Coupe	
50-B	Sport Coupe	
55-B	Tudor Sedan	
68-B	Cabriolet	
155-C	Town Sedan	(Murray)
155-D	Town Sedan	(Briggs)
165-C	Standard Ford or Sedan	(Murray)
165-D	Standard Ford or Sedan	(Briggs)
170-B	Standard Ford or Sedan	two-window
170-B	DeLuxe Ford or Sedan	two-window
180-A	DeLuxe Phaeton	
190-A	Victoria	
78-A	Pickup Truck	
79-A	Panel Delivery	
79-B	Panel Delivery	
85-A	Panel Delivery	
130-A	DeLuxe Delivery	
130-B	DeLuxe Delivery Drop Floor	
150-A	Station Wagon	
225-A	Panel Delivery Drop Floor	
180-A	DeLuxe Phaeton	

1931

Model Number	Name	Description
35-B	Standard Phaeton	
40-B	Standard Roadster	
40-B	DeLuxe Roadster	
45-B	Standard Coupe	
45-B	DeLuxe Coupe	
50-B	Sport Coupe	
55-B	Tudor Sedan	
68-B	Cabriolet	
68-C	Cabriolet	
155-C	Town Sedan	(Murray)
155-D	Town Sedan	(Briggs)
160-A	Standard Ford or Sedan	
160-B	Town Sedan	
160-C	Fordor DeLuxe Sedan	
165-C	Standard Ford or Sedan	(Murray)
165-D	Standard Ford or Sedan	(Briggs)
170-B	DeLuxe Ford or Sedan	two-window
180-A	DeLuxe Phaeton	
190-A	Victoria	
66-A	DeLuxe Pickup Truck	
78-A	Pickup Truck	
78-B	Pickup Truck	
79-A	Panel Delivery	103.5in wheelbase
79-B	Panel Delivery	103.5in wheelbase
130-B	DeLuxe Delivery Drop Floor	
130-B	DeLuxe Delivery Regular Floor	
150-B	Station Wagon	
400-A	Convertible Sedan	
300-A	DeLuxe Delivery	
280-A	Ambulance	
285-A	DeLuxe Police Patrol	
290-A	Standard Police Patrol	
295-A	Town Car Delivery	
255-A	Special Natural Wood Delivery	
225-A	Panel Delivery Drop Floor	
270-A	Funeral Service	
275-A	Funeral Coach	
65-A	Canopy and Screen Pickup Truck	
76-B	Open Cab Pickup Truck	
196-A	Canopy Top and Screen Pickup Truck	
198-A	Canopy Top and Screen Pickup Truck	
180-A	DeLuxe Phaeton	

Specifications

Model T
Wheelbase: 100in
Overall length:
  Bare chassis, 128in
  Car body, 134.5in
  Weight: 1200lb
Engine:
  L-head
  Cast-iron block
  176.7ci
  Solid valve lifters
  Bore and Stroke, 3 3/4inx4in
  Compression ratio, 4.5:1
  Horsepower, 22bhp at 1600rpm (1908-1912); 20bhp at 1600rpm (1913-1927)
Tires:
  Front, 30x3in
  Rear, 30x3 1/2in
  Tread: Front, 56in; Rear, 60in (Optional until 1916)

Model A 1928-1929
Wheelbase: 103.5in
Weight:
  Low, 2050lb (1928 Business Roadster);
  High, 2386lb (1928 Fordor Sedan)
  Low, 2100lb (1929 Roadster);
  High, 2525lb (1929 Town Car)
Engine:
  L-head, four-cylinder
  Cast-iron block
  200.5ci
  Bore and Stroke, 3 7/8inx4 1/4in
  Compression ratio, 4.22:1
  Torque, 128lb/ft at 1000rpm
  Horsepower, 40bhp at 2200rpm
  Carburetor, Holley or Zenith 2V
Transmission:
  Sliding gears
  Standard "H" pattern
  Three forward speeds, one reverse speed
Rear axle ratio: 3.70:1
Tires: 4.50inx21in
Wheels: 21in
Tread: Front/Rear, 56in

Model A 1930-1931
Weight:
  Low, 2155lb (1930-1931 Standard Roadster);
  High, 2500lb (1930-1931 Station Wagon)
Engine: Same as 1928-1929
Transmission: Same as 1928-1929
Rear end ratio: 3.77:1
Tires: 4.75inx19in
Wheels: 19in

Clubs

Model A Restorers Club
24800 Michigan Ave.
Dearborn, MI 48124

The Model A Restorers Club publishes a nice bimonthly magazine called the *Model A News*, that is full of Model A information. Regional chapters are located throughout the United States, as well as in foreign countries. Dues are $15 per year for US residents and $16 per year outside of the United States.

Model A Ford Club of America
250 S. Cypress
La Habra, CA 90631-5586

Formed in 1955, the Model A Ford Club of America is one of the largest marque clubs in the world. It publishes a bimonthly club magazine called the *Restorer*. Chapters are located throughout the United States and in foreign countries. Dues are $20 per year for US residents and $24 per year outside of the United States.

Model T Ford Club International
P.O. Box 438315
Chicago, IL 60643-8315

During the late 1940s and early 1950s, a group of Model T enthusiasts decided to form a club and share their enthusiasm. In 1952, they banded together and formed the Model T Ford Club International. Since that time, the club has grown to encompass seventy-three chapters worldwide. It publishes a bimonthly magazine called the *Model T Times*. Membership for US residents is $20 per year and $23 per year outside of the United States.

Model T Ford Club of America
P.O. Box 7400
Burbank, CA 91510

Founded in 1965, this club is dedicated to promoting and enjoying Model T Fords. Contact club for further details.

Model T and Model A Reading Materials

Ford, the Dust and Glory: A Racing History. Leo Levine. MacMillan & Company, New York, NY. 1968. Racing history of Ford cars from the #999 all the way to Le Mans of 1967. Out of print.

Ford Model T Scrapbook. Floyd Clymer. Clymer Publications, 1955 (?). Lots of Model T Ford information and photographs.

From Here to Obscurity. Ray Miller and Bruce McCalley. Evergreen Press, Oceanside, CA, 1972. The story of the Model T in pictures.

Henry Ford. Regina Z. Kelly. Follett Publishing Company, Chicago Il, 1970. Hardbound book about Henry Ford and the cars he built. Out of print.

Henry Ford and Grass Roots America. Reynold M. Wik. University of Michigan Press, 1972. Hardbound book which traces the history of Ford and the effect Henry Ford had on America.

Henry Ford, Great Lives Observed. Edited by John B. Rae. Prentice Hall Publishing, Spectrum Books, Englewood Cliffs, NJ, 1969. Henry Ford's life, his company, and his cars.

Henry Ford, People of Destiny. Kenneth Richards. Children's Press, Chicago, IL, 1967. A good book about Henry Ford and his cars written for children.

Henry's Lady. Ray Miller. Evergreen Press, Oceanside, CA, 1972. Covers all Model A years from 1928 through 1931. Lots of photographs show details and differences between models and model years.

Henry's Model T. Automobile Quarterly Publications, 10:/4, 1973. Articles and photographs of Model T Fords.

How to Restore Your Model A Ford. Model A Ford Club of America. Published by the Model A Ford Club of America, La Habra, CA. Articles on restoration reprinted from the club's magazines.

Illustrated Ford Pickup Truck Buyer's Guide. Paul G. McLaughlin. Motorbooks International, Osceola, WI, 1991. Softbound book covering all light-duty commercial vehicles built by Ford from 1905 to 1991. Lots of Model T and Model A pickup coverage.

Illustrated History of Ford. Crestline Publishing, Glen Ellyn, IL, 1970. This hardbound book covers Ford cars and trucks from 1903 through 1970. Lots of text and black-and-white photos of popular Ford models.

Model A Ford Paint and Finish Guide. Model A Ford Club of America. Published by the Model A Ford Club of America, La Habra, CA. This book tells you how to paint, and what colors were available on Model A Fords: color schemes, pinstripes, etc.

Model A Judging Standards and Restoration Guidelines 1928-1931. Model A Ford Club of America and the Model A Restorers Club. Published by the Model A Ford Club of America, La Habra, CA. If you are looking to restore a Model A by the book to compete successfully in car shows this is the book you need.

Model A Miseries and Cures. Mary Moline. Rumbleseat Press, Van Nuys, CA 1972. Lots of good Model A information; a must for the Model A enthusiast.

Model T Restoration Handbook. Leslie R. Henry. Polly Print, Nashville, TN, 1971. A fully illustrated complete restoration guide from a noted authority on the subject.

Model T Service and Shop Manual. Published originally by Ford Motor Company. Reprint of original Model T service manuals.

Ninety Years of Ford. George Dammann. Motorbooks International, Osceola, WI, 1993. Updated version of Dammann's 1970 *Illustrated History of Ford.* Includes more than two more decades of material which the Ford enthusiast will find interesting.

The American Ford. Lorin Sorensen. Silverado Publishing, St. Helena, CA, 1975. Large-format photographic history of products built by Ford. Lots of black-and-white factory photos used throughout.

The Best of Ford. Mary Moline. Rumbleseat Press, Van Nuys, CA, 1973. An enjoyable collection of stories about Ford and the cars he built.

The Ford Road, 1903-1978. Lorin Sorensen. Silverado Publishing, St. Helena, CA, 1978. Hardbound book full of vintage photos released during Ford's seventy-fifth anniversary celebrations.

The Model T Ford Owner. Murray Fahnestock. Lincoln Publishing, Lockport, NY, 1983. Everything you ever wanted to know about the Model T Ford from a technical and performance standpoint.

The Open Fords. Lorin Sorensen. Silverado Publishing, St. Helena, 1979. Large-format photographic history of the open Fords.

Wheels for a Nation. Frank Donovan. Thomas Crowell Publishing, 1965. Model T information.

Sources

Alabama
Good Old Days Garage
2340 Farley Place
Birmingham, AL 35226
205-822-4569
   Model T and Model A engines

Arizona
Chuck Cubel
P.O. Box 3924
Apache Junction, AZ 85217
602-983-6785
   Replacement wood pieces for Model Ts and Model As

California
Antique Automotive
2451 State St.
San Diego, CA 92101
800-995-6626
Model A parts

Butler's T Service
1209 Delaware St., #1
Huntington Beach, CA 92648
714-960-5704
   Model T and Model A engine and transmission rebuilding

Kim Dobbins
1707 W. 265th St.
Harbor City, CA 90710
310-539-9328
   Early Model T parts

Mal's A Sales
4966 S. Pacheco Blvd.
Martinez, CA 94553
510-228-8180
   Model A parts

Rootlieb Inc.
815 S. Soderquist
Turlock, CA 95380
209-632-2203
   Model T Speedster kits

Sacramento Vintage Parts
4675 Aldona Ln.
Sacramento, CA 95841
916-489-3444
   Model A parts

Specialty Ford Parts
9103 Garvey
Rosemead, CA 91770
   Model A parts

Connecticut
As and More
Box 165
Stafford, CT 06075
203-684-6532
   Model A parts

Vintage Glass
40 Kingsbury
Tolland, CT 06084
800-727-5584
   Model A wind wings and other Model A glass

Yesterday's Auto Parts
P.O. Box 1723
Lakeville, CT 06039
203-435-4933
   Model A parts

Georgia
Mike's Model A Parts
1930 Patrick Road
Dacula, GA 30211
404-945-3671
   Model A parts

Illinois
Arnold Levin
2634 Woodlawn Rd.
Northbrook, IL 60062
   Model T carbide generators

Bob's Antique Auto Parts
7826 Forest Hills Road
Rockford, IL 61132
815-633-7244
   Model T parts

Ernie Hemmings Bookseller
Box 3906-H
Quincy, IL 62305
   Model T and Model A books

Indiana
McDonald Parts Co.
R.R. 3, Box 94
Rockport, IN 47653
812-359-5555
   FoMoCo script glass for Model As

Iowa
Hudson Wagon Works
Rt. 1, Box 28
Bridgewater, IA 50837
515-369-2865
   Huckster wagons, Depot Hacks, and other wooden bodies

Les Anderson
1235 Nash Ave.
Kanawha, IA 50447
515-762-3528
   Model T coils rebuilt

Norm's Antique Auto Supply
1921 Hickory Grove
Davenport, IA 52804
319-322-8388
   Used Model A parts

Kansas
Amett Obsolete Parts
308 Pedigo
Pratt, KS 67124
316-672-9241
   Used Model T parts

Easy Jacks & Sons
2725 S. Milford Lake Rd.
Junction City, KS 66441-8446
913-238-7541
   Used Model T and Model A parts

Mark Freimiller
R.R. 3
Iola, KS 66749
316-365-6709
   Used Model T parts

Louisiana
American Antique Auto Parts
3612 W. Louisiana State Dr.
Kenner, LA 70065
504-467-1614
   Model T and Model A parts

Maryland
Bratton's Antique Auto Parts
9410 Watkins Rd.
Gaithersburg, MD 20882
800-255-1929
   Model A parts

Massachusetts
Carl A. King
59 Adams Ave.
Everett, MA 02149
   Magazine ads for Model Ts, Model As, and other Fords

Ezolds Model A Garage
126 Long Pond Rd.
Westfield, MA 01085
413-532-8839
    Rebuilding services for Model As

Freeman's Garage
19 Freeman St.
Norton, MA 02766
508-285-6500
    Model A servicing and restoration work

J & M Machine Shop
40 Mt. Vickery Rd.
Southborough, MA 01772
508-460-0733
    Model T and Model A engine rebuilding

Lang's Model T Parts
P.O. Box 7
Ashburnham, MA 01430
800-872-7871
    Model T parts

LeBaron Bonney Co.
P.O. Box 6
6 Chestnut St.
Amesbury, MA 01913
508-388-3811
    Model A interior and top kits

Mike and Ed Stein
31 Gilbert Rd.
Southampton, MA 01073
413-527-5129
    Model T and Model A engine rebuilding

Pioneer Valley Model A
81 East St.
Easthampton, MA 01027
413-584-8400
    Model A restoration services

PV Antique Ford Parts
1688 Main St.
Tewksbury, MA 01876
508-851-9159
    Model A parts

Michigan
Harkos Model A Parts
13245 Northline
Southgate, MI 48195
313-283-3511
    Model A parts

Little Dearborn Parts
2424 SE University Ave.
Minneapolis, MN 55414
612-331-2066
    Model T and Model A restoration and street rod parts

Missouri
Battlefield Antique Parts
5054 S. Broadview
Battlefield, MO 65619
417-882-7923
    Model A parts

Dan Bixby
Rt. 1, Box 565
Bismarck, MO 63624
314-734-2308
    Model A parts

Montana
Montana Collector Cars
Box 305
Dutton, MT 59433
    Model T cars and parts

Nebraska
Mike Dennis
Nebraska Ford Parts
1845 S. 48th
Lincoln, NE 68506
402-489-3036
    Model A parts

New York
Anderson
70 Coleman Rd.
Jamestown, NY 14701
716-484-3141
    Rebuilt Model T parts

Fichen Auto Parts
132 Calvert Ave.
West Babylon, NY 11704
516-587-3332
    Trico windshield wiper parts

Heritage Automotive Restorations
36 River Rd.
Pawling, NY 12564
    Model T and Model A restorations

Joblot Automotive
98-11 211th St.
Queens Village, NY 11429
718-468-8585
    1928-1931 Model A parts

Ken Bialynski
4949 Ridge Rd.
Williamson, NY 14589
315-483-2650
    Model T racer parts

Mac's Antique Auto Parts
1051 Lincoln Ave.
Lockport, NY 14094
800-777-0948
    Model T and Model A parts

Pleasantville Manufacturing Co.
R.R. 1, Box 89
Dewittville, NY 14728
    Model A Woody Wagon bodies

Restore-It Antique Auto Parts
314 Park Ave.
Mechanicville, NY 12118
518-664-3481
    Model A parts

Ohio
Donald Shively
Rt. 4
Wheelersburg, OH 45694
614-574-6068
    Model T and Model A parts

Funk's Antique Auto Parts
330 Industry Dr.
Carlisle, OH 45005
513-746-1113
    Reproduction Model A parts

Gaslight Auto Parts
P.O. Box 291
Urbana, OH 43078
513-652-2147
    Model T and Model A parts

John Gamble
1639 Marion Waldo Rd., #66
Marion, OH 43302
614-389-4044
    Model T carburetors

Lloyd's Literature
Box 491
Newbury, OH 44065
216-338-1527
    Model A/Model T manuals, sales literature

Snyder's Antique Auto Parts
12925 Woodworth Rd.
New Sprigfield, OH 44443
216-549-5313
    Model T and Model A parts

Oklahoma
Obsolete Ford Parts
8701 S. Interstate 35
Oklahoma City, OK 73149
405-631-3933
    Model T and Model A parts

Vernon Bliss
R.R. 1, Box 74
Freedom, OK 73842
405-621-3354
    Model T and Model A parts

Oregon
Bob Drake Reproductions
1819 NW Washington Blvd.
Grant's Pass, OR 97526
800-221-3673
    1928-1929 Model A steering wheels

Jerry Bougher Ads
3628 SE Union St.
Albany, OR 97321
    Model Ts, Model As, and other Ford magazine ads

M & S Hydraulics
22275 SW TV Hwy.
Hillsboro, OR 97123
503-642-1122
    New and rebuilt Model A shocks

Mumby's Model A Wood Kits
13095 SW Butner Ct.
Beaverton, OR 97005
503-646-5900
    Model A wood kits

Plameter Corporation
173 SE Queen Ave.
Albany, OR 97321
503-928-3233
   Model A brake drums

The Model A Works
3970 N. Interstate 5
Portland, OR 97227
503-284-1928
   K.R. Wilson reproduction tools for Model As and Model Ts

Rhode Island
Rhode Island Wiring Service
Box 434H
West Kingston, RI 02892
401-789-1955
   Wiring looms for Model Ts and Model As

Texas
Howell's Sheet Metal Co.
P.O. Box 179
Nome, TX 77629
409-253-2478
   Model T and Model A sheet metal parts

Jay Ketelle
3721 Farwell
Amarillo, TX 79109
   Auto literature, including that for Model Ts and Model As

Ken Perkins
401 S. Grove
Richardson, TX 75081
   Rebuilt Ford speedometers, Model A tool kits

Performance Antique Parts
P.O. Box 669
Dickinson, TX 77539
713-337-3033
   Model T engines and performance parts

Siemering
400 Pecan Bend, #372
Bedford, TX 76022
817-285-7083
   Model A sheet metal

Virginia
PJ's Antique Fords
Rt. 7, Box 7050
Gloucester, VA 23061
804-693-4332
   Model A radiators

Wisconsin
Classic Motorbooks
P.O. Box 1, Osceola, WI
715-294-3345
   Books and videotapes for the automobile enthusiast

Index

Branch offices, 25
Deluxe line, 81
Eagle boats, 24
Edison, Thomas Alva, 78
Fairbanks, Douglas, 64
Farkas, Eugene, 63
Ford Motor Company, 6,
Ford Motor Company Ltd., 11
Ford Motor Company Plants, 9, 11, 16, 17, 19, 20, 30, 33, 39, 43, 53, 76, 83, 96
Ford, Edsel, 23, 24, 33, 38, 62, 63, 92, 103
Ford, Henry II, 33
Ford, Henry, 6, 7, 9-11, 16, 17, 19, 20, 22, 24, 29, 30, 33, 35, 38, 39, 51, 55, 62, 63, 67, 72, 73, 76, 78, 97, 103
Fordson tractor, 23
Galamb, Joe, 63
Johnson, Frank, 63
Knudsen, William, S., 39
Kulick, Frank, 43
Leland, Henry, 37, 38
Martin, Peter, 63
Model A, 55, 62-106
Model K Roadster, 7
Model K Touring Car, 8
Model N Runabout, 7
Model R Runabout, 7
Model S Runabout, 7
Model T, 7-62, 64, 65, 102-106
One-ton truck, 22
Pickford, Mary, 64
Pickup Truck, 51, 67, 80, 94
Races, 9, 43, 68
Sheldrick, Lawrence, 63
Sorensen, Charlie, 63
Standard line, 81
The Dearborn Independent, 30

Model T models
Center Door Sedan, 19, 42
Commercial Roadster, 11, 13
Commercial Runabout, 11
Coupe, 8, 12, 37, 43, 51, 53
Coupelet, 17, 23
Delivery Car, 11, 13
Fordor Sedan, 42, 51, 53
Foredoor Touring Car, 12
Landaulet, 8
Open Front Touring Cars, 12, 16, 17, 19
Roadsters, 16, 43
Runabout, 8, 12, 16, 37, 51, 53
Stripped down one-ton chassis, 22
Stripped-down chassis , 13
Taxicab, 19
Torpedo Roadster, 12, 13
Torpedo Runabout, 9
Tourabout, 8
Touring Car, 8, 12, 43, 51, 53
Town Car, 8, 12, 13
Tudor Sedan, 42, 51

Model A models
Cabriolet, 73, 75, 94
Canopy Top Pickup Truck, 94
Closed-Cab Pickup Truck, 67, 75
Commercial Pickup Truck, 64
Convertible Sedan, 93, 94
Coupe, 64, 75
DeLuxe Coupe, 96
DeLuxe Delivery Car, 73, 93
DeLuxe Fordor Sedan, 94
DeLuxe Phaeton, 82, 96
DeLuxe Pickup Truck, 94
DeLuxe Roadster, 94
DeLuxe Tudor, 94
Drop Floor Panel Delivery, 94
Fordor Sedan, 64, 75
Model AA trucks, 67
Natural Wood Panel Delivery, 93, 94
Panel Delivery, 94
Panel Truck, 67
Phaeton Touring Car, 67
Phaeton, 64, 75
Roadster Pickup Truck, 75
Roadster, 64, 75
Sedan Delivery, 75
Special Business Coupe, 67
Special Delivery, 94
Sport Coupe with Rumble Seat, 64, 67
Sport Coupe, 75
Standard Coupe, 96
Standard Phaeton, 82, 94
Standard Roadster, 94
Standard Tudor, 96
Station Wagon, 73, 75, 80, 93, 94
Taxicab, 73, 75
Town Car Delivery, 82, 83, 93
Town Car DeLuxe, 94
Town Car, 75, 76, 82
Town Sedan, 75, 94
Tudor Sedan, 64, 75, 83
Victoria, 82, 94, 96